"Hey, Whipple, Squeeze This."

Adweek Books is designed to present interesting, insightful books for the general business reader and for professionals in the worlds of media, marketing, and advertising.

These are innovative, creative books that address the challenges and opportunities of these industries, written by leaders in the business. Some of our writers head their own companies, others have worked their way up to the top of their field in large multinationals. But they share a knowledge of their craft and a desire to enlighten others.

We hope readers will find these books as helpful and inspiring as *Adweek,* *Brandweek,* and *Mediaweek* magazines.

Published

Disruption: Overturning Conventions and Shaking Up the Marketplace, Jean Marie-Dru

"Hey, Whipple, Squeeze This.": A Guide to Creating Great Ads, Luke Sullivan

Truth, Lies & Advertising: The Art of Account Planning, Jon Steel

Under the Radar: Talking to Today's Cynical Consumer, Jonathan Bond & Richard Kirshenbaum

Forthcoming

Eating the Big Fish: How "Challenger Brands" Can Compete Against Brand Leaders, Adam Morgan

"Hey, Whipple, Squeeze This."

A Guide to Creating Great Ads

LUKE SULLIVAN

John Wiley & Sons, Inc.

New York • Chichester • Weinheim • Brisbane • Singapore • Toronto

This text is printed on acid-free paper.

Copyright © 1998 by Luke Sullivan
Published by John Wiley & Sons, Inc.

All rights reserved. Published simultaneously in Canada.

Library of Congress Cataloging-in-Publication Data:

Sullivan, Luke.
    "Hey, Whipple, squeeze this." : a guide to creating great ads /
Luke Sullivan.
      p.   cm.—(Adweek books)
    Includes bibliographical references and index.
    ISBN 0-471-29339-3 (alk. paper)
    1. Advertising copy. I. Title. II. Series.
HF5825.S88   1998
659.13′2—dc21   97-31678
                                        CIP

Printed in the United States of America
10 9 8 7

TO MY DEAR WIFE,

CURLIN,

AND OUR LITTLE BOYS,

REED AND PRESTON

CONTENTS

PREFACE

THIS IS MY FANTASY.

———

We open on a tidy suburban kitchen. Actually, it's a room off the side, one with a washer and dryer. On the floor is a basketful of laundry. The camera closes in.

Out of the laundry pops the cutest little stuffed bear you've ever seen. He's pink and fluffy, has a happy little face, and there's one sock stuck adorably to his left ear.

"Hi, I'm Snuggles, the fabric-softening bear. And I . . ."

The first bullet rips into Snuggles' stomach, blows out of his back in a blizzard of cotton entrails, and punches a fist-sized hole in the dryer behind. Snuggles grabs the side of the Rubbermaid laundry basket and sinks down, his plastic eyes rolling as he looks for the source of the gunfire.

Taking cover behind 1/16 inch of flexible acrylic rubber, Snuggles looks out of the basket's plastic mesh and into the living room. He sees nothing. The dining room. Nothing.

Snuggles is easing over the back side of the basket when the second shot takes his head off at the neck. His body lands on top of the laundry, which is remarkably soft and fluffy. Fade to black.

━━━━━━━━

We open on a woman in a bathroom, clad in apron and wielding brush, poised to clean her toilet bowl. She opens the lid.

But wait. What's this? It's a little man in a boat, floating above the sparkling waters of Lake Porcelain. Everything looks clean already!

With a tip of his teeny hat, he introduces himself. "I'm the Ty-D-Bowl Man, and I . . ."

Both hat and hand disappear as the first bullet screams through and blows a hole in curved toilet wall behind the Ty-D-Bowl Man. Water begins to pour out on the floor as the woman screams and dives for cover in the tub.

Ty-D-Bowl Man scrambles out of the bowl, but when he climbs onto the big silver lever, it gives way, dropping him back into the swirling waters of the flushing toilet. We get two more glimpses of his face as he orbits around, once, twice, and then down to his final reward.

━━━━━━━━

We open on a grocery store, where we see the owner scolding a group of ladies for squeezing some toilet paper. The first shot is high and wide, shattering a jar of mayonnaise.

"Hey, Whipple, Squeeze This."

Figure 1.1   Whipple.

1

Salesmen Don't Have to Wear Plaid

Selling without selling out

I GREW UP POINTING A FINGER-GUN at Mr. Whipple. He kept interrupting my favorite shows. The morning lineup was my favorite, with its back-to-back *Dick Van Dyke* and *Andy Griffith* shows. But Whipple kept butting in on Rob and Laura Petrie.

He'd appear uninvited on my TV, looking over the top of his glasses and pursing his lips at the ladies in his grocery store. Two middle-aged women, presumably with high school or college degrees, would be standing in the aisle squeezing rolls of toilet paper. Whipple would wag his finger and scold, "Please don't squeeze the Charmin." After the ladies scurried away, he'd give the rolls a few furtive squeezes himself.

I used to shoot him the second he appeared, but later discovered greater satisfaction in waiting till the 27th second, when *he* was squeezing the Charmin. *Bang!* and he was gone.

Now, years later, I am armed like millions of other Americans with a remote control. I still go looking for Whipple, and if I see him, I'm takin' him out.

To be fair, Procter & Gamble's Charmin commercials weren't the worst thing that ever aired on television. They had a concept, though contrived, and a brand image, though irritating, even to a ninth grader.

If it were just me who didn't like Whipple's commercials, well, I might write it off. But the more I read on the campaign, the more consensus I discovered. In Martin Mayer's book, *Whatever Happened to Madison Avenue?*, I found this:

> [Charmin's Whipple was] one of the most disliked . . . television commercials of the 1970s. [E]verybody thought "Please don't squeeze the Charmin" was stupid and it ranked last in believability in all the commercials studied for a period of years . . .[1]

In a book called *How to Advertise*, I found:

> When asked which campaigns they most disliked, consumers convicted Mr. Whipple . . . Charmin may have not been popular advertising, but it was number one in sales.[2]

And *there* is the crux of the problem. The mystery. How did Whipple's commercials sell so much toilet paper?

These shrill little interruptions that irritated nearly everyone, that were used as fodder for Johnny Carson on late-night TV, sold toilet paper by the ton. How? Even if you figure that part out, the question then becomes, why? Why would you irritate your buying public with a twittering, pursed-lipped grocer when cold, hard research told you everybody hated him? I don't get it.

Apparently, even the agency that created him didn't get it. John Lyons, author of *Guts—Advertising from the Inside Out*, worked at Charmin's agency when they were trying to figure out what to do with Whipple.

> I was assigned to assassinate Mr. Whipple. Some of New York's best hit teams before me had tried and failed. "Killing Whipple" was an ongoing mission at Benton & Bowles. The agency that created him was determined to kill him. But the question was how to knock off a man with 15 lives, one for every year that the . . . campaign had been running at the time.[3]

No idea he came up with ever replaced Whipple, Lyons noted.

Next up to assassinate Whipple, a young writer, Atlanta's Joey Reiman. In a phone conversation, Reiman told me he tried to sell P&G a concept called "Squeeze-Enders"—an Alcoholics Anonymous kind of group where troubled souls struggled to end their visits to Mr. Whipple's grocery store, and so perhaps end the Whipple dynasty. No sale. Procter & Gamble wasn't about to let go of a winner. Whipple remained for years as one of advertising's most bulletproof personalities.

As well he should have. He was selling literally billions of rolls of toilet paper. *Billions.* In 1975, a survey listed Whipple as the second-most-recognized face in America, right behind Richard Nixon. When Benton & Bowles' creative director, Al Hampel, took Whipple (a great character actor named Dick Wilson) to dinner one night in New York City, he said "it was as if Robert Redford walked into the place. Even the waiters asked for autographs."

So on one hand you had research telling you customers hated these repetitive, schmaltzy, cornball commercials. And on the other, you had Whipple signing autographs at the Four Seasons.

It was as if the whole scenario came out of the '40s. In Fred Wakeman's 1946 novel, *The Hucksters,* this was how advertising worked. In the middle of a meeting, the client spat on the conference-room table and said: "You have just seen me do a disgusting thing. Ugly word, spit. But you'll always remember what I just did."[4]

The account executive in the novel took the lesson, later musing: "It was working like magic. The more you irritated them with repetitious commercials, the more soap they bought."[5]

With 504 different Charmin toilet tissue commercials airing from 1964 through 1990, Procter & Gamble certainly "irritated them with repetitious commercials." And it indeed "worked like magic." P&G knew what they were doing.

Yet I lie awake some nights staring at the ceiling, troubled by Whipple. What vexes me so about this old grocer? This is the question that led me to write this book.

What troubles me about Whipple is that he isn't *good.* As an idea, Whipple isn't good.

He may have been an effective salesman. (Billions of rolls.) He may have been a strong brand image. (He knocked Scott tissues out of the #1 spot.) But it all comes down to this: If I had created Mr. Whipple, I don't think I could tell my son with a straight face what I did at the office. "Well, son, you see, Whipple tells the lady shoppers not to squeeze the Charmin but then, then he squeezes it *himself*. . . . Hey, wait, come back."

As an idea, Whipple isn't good.

To those who defend the campaign based on sales, I ask, would you also spit on the table to get my attention? It would work, but would you? An eloquent gentleman named Norman Berry, a British creative director at Ogilvy & Mather, put it this way:

> I'm appalled by those who [judge] advertising exclusively on the basis of sales. That isn't enough. Of course, advertising must sell. By any definition it is lousy advertising if it doesn't. But if sales are achieved with work which is in bad taste or is intellectual garbage, it shouldn't be applauded no matter how much it sells. Offensive, dull, abrasive, stupid advertising is bad for the entire industry and bad for business as a whole. It is why the public perception of advertising is going down in this country.[6]

Berry may well have been thinking of Mr. Whipple when he made that comment in the early '80s. With every year that's passed since, newer and more virulent strains of vapidity have been created: Ring Around the Collar—Snuggles, the fabric-softening bear—Toyota, I love what you do for me—He loves my mind *and* he drinks Johnny Walker Red—Don't hate me because I'm beautiful—I'm not a doctor, but I play one on TV—I bring home the bacon, I fry it up in a pan, and I never, ever let him forget he's a man.

Writer Fran Lebowitz may well have been watching TV when she observed: "No matter how cynical I get, it's impossible to keep up."

Certainly, the viewing public is cynical about our business, due almost entirely to this parade of idiots we've sent into their living rooms. Every year, as long as I've been in advertising, Gallup publishes their poll of most- and least-trusted professions. And every year, advertising practitioners trade last or second-to-last place with used-car salesmen and members of Congress.

It reminds me of a paragraph I plucked from our office bulletin board, one of those xeroxed curiosities that makes its way around corporate America:

Dear Ann: I have a problem. I have two brothers. One brother is in advertising. The other was put to death in the electric chair for murder. My mother died from insanity when I was three years old. My two sisters are prostitutes and my father sells narcotics to grade school students. Recently, I met a girl who was just released from a reformatory where she served time for killing her dog with a ball-peen hammer, and I want to marry her. My problem is, should I tell her about my brother who is in advertising? Signed, Anonymous.

"THE CUSTOMER IS NOT A MORON.
HE IS YOUR HUSBAND."

My problem with Whipple (effective sales, grating execution) isn't a new one. In 1949, it occurred to a gentleman named William Bernbach that a commercial needn't sacrifice wit, grace, or intelligence in order to increase sales.

Bill Bernbach founded his New York agency, Doyle Dane Bernbach, on the then radical notion that customers aren't nitwits who need to be fooled or lectured or hammered into listening to a client's sales message. This is Bill Bernbach:

> The truth isn't the truth until people believe you, and they can't believe you if they don't know what you're saying, and they can't know what you're saying if they don't listen to you, and they won't listen to you if you're not interesting, and you won't be interesting unless you say things imaginatively, originally, freshly.[7]

The classic Bernbach paradigm.

From all the advertising texts, articles, speeches, and awards annuals I've read over my years in advertising, everything that's any good about this business seems to trace its heritage back to this man, William Bernbach—creativity's ground zero. And when his agency landed a couple of highly visible national accounts like Volkswagen and Alka-Seltzer, he brought advertising into a new era.

Smart agencies and clients everywhere saw for themselves that advertising didn't have to embarrass itself in order to make a cash register ring. The national TV audience was eating it up. Viewers couldn't wait for the next airing of VW's "Funeral" or Alka-Seltzer's

"Spicy meatball." The first shots of the Creative Revolution of the '60s had been fired.*

How marvelous to have actually *been* there when DDB art director, Helmut Krone, laid out one of the very first Volkswagen ads (Fig. 1.2). A black-and-white picture of that simple car, no women draped over the fender, no mansion in the background. A one-word headline: "Lemon." And the simple, self-effacing copy that began: "This Volkswagen missed the boat. The chrome strip on the glove compartment is blemished and must be replaced. Chances are you wouldn't have noticed it; Inspector Kurt Kroner did."

Maybe this ad doesn't seem earth-shattering now; we've all seen our share of great advertising since then. But remember, DDB first did this when other car companies were running headlines like: "Blue ribbon beauty that's stealing the thunder from the high-priced cars!" And "Chevrolet's 3 new engines put new fun under your foot and a great big grin on your face!" Volkswagen's was a totally new voice.

Then came the 1970s. The tightening economy had middle managers everywhere scared. And the party ended as quickly as it had begun.

The new gods wore suits and came bearing calculators. Research blew into the business like your dad into a high school keg party. *"Enough of this Kreativity Krap-ola, my little scribblers. We're here to meet the client's numbers. Put 'new' in that headline. Drop that concept and pick up an adjective: Crunch-a-licious, Flavor-iffic, I don't care. The client's coming up the elevator. Chop, chop."*

In *Corporate Report,* columnist William Souder wrote:

> Creative departments were reined in. New ads were pre-tested in focus groups, and subsequent audience-penetration and consumer-awareness quotients were numbingly monitored. It seemed that with enough repetition, even the most strident ad campaigns could bore through to the public consciousness. Advertising turned shrill. People hated Mr. Whipple, but bought Charmin anyway. It was Wisk for Ring-Around-The-Collar and Sanka for your jangled nerves.[8]

---

*You can study these two seminal commercials and many other great ads from this era in Larry Dubrow's fine book on the Creative Revolution, *When Advertising Tried Harder,* New York: Friendly Press, 1984.

Figure 1.2   In the beginning, there was the word. And it was "Lemon."

And so even after a decade full of brilliant, successful examples like Volkswagen, Avis, Polaroid, and Chivas Regal, the pendulum swung back to the dictums of research. The industry returned to the blaring jingles and crass gimmickry of decades previous. The wolf was at the door again. Wearing a suit.

Such was the state of the business when I joined its ranks in 1979.

The battle between these opposing forces of hot creativity and cold research rages to this hour. It makes for an interesting day at the office. John Ward of England's B&B Dorland noted, "Advertising is a craft executed by people who aspire to be artists, but [is] assessed by those who aspire to be scientists. I cannot imagine any human relationship more perfectly designed to produce total mayhem."[9]

WELCOME TO ADVERTISING.
GRAB AN ADJECTIVE.

When I was in seventh grade, I noticed something about the ads for cereal on TV. (Remember, this was before the FTC forced manufacturers to call these sugary puffs of crunchy air "*part* of a complete breakfast.") I noticed the cereals were looking more and more like candy. There were flocks of leprechauns or birds or bees flying around the bowl, dusting sparkles of sugar over the cereal or ladling on gooey rivers of chocolate-flavored coating. The food value of the product kept getting less important until it was finally stuffed into the trunk of the car and sugar moved into the driver's seat. It was all about sugar.

One morning in study hall, I drew this little progression (Fig. 1.3), calling it "History of a Cereal Box."

I was interested in the advertising I saw on TV but never thought I'd take it up as a career. I liked to draw, to make comic books, and to doodle with words and pictures. But when I was a poor college student, all I was sure of was that I wanted to be "rich." I went into the premed program.

The first grade on my college transcript, for chemistry, was a big, fat, radioactive "F." I reconsidered.

I majored in psychology. But after college I couldn't find any businesses on Lake Street in Minneapolis that were hiring skinny chain-smokers who could explain the relative virtues of scheduled versus random reinforcement in behaviorist theory. I joined a construction crew.

When the opportunity to be an editor/typesetter/ad salesperson for a small neighborhood newspaper came along, I took it, at a salary of $80 every two weeks. (I thought I deserved $85.) But the

*Figure 1.3 False advertising doesn't fool anybody, even seventh graders.
When I was 12, I was irritated by all the cereal commercials featuring
"sugar sparkles" and drew this progression of cereal box designs.*

opportunity to sit at a desk and use words to make a living was enough. Of all my duties, I found that selling ads and "drawing them up" were the most interesting.

For the next year and a half, I hovered around the edges of the advertising industry. I did pasteup for another small newsweekly and then put in a long and dreary stint as a typesetter in the ad department of a large department store. It was there, during a break from setting type about "thick and thirsty cotton bath towels: $9.99," that I first came upon a book featuring the winners of a local advertising-awards show.

I was bowled over by the work I saw there—mostly campaigns from Tom McElligott and Ron Anderson from Bozell & Jacobs' Minneapolis office. Their ads didn't say "thick and thirsty cotton bath towels: $9.99." They were funny or they were serious—startling sometimes—but they were always intelligent.

Reading one of their ads felt like I'd just met a very likable person at a bus stop. *He's smart, he's funny, he doesn't talk about himself. Turns out he's a salesman. And he's selling? . . . Well, wouldn't you know it, I've been thinking about buying one of those. Maybe I'll give you a call. Bye. Walking away you think, nice enough fella. And the way he said things: so funny.*

Through a contact, I managed to get a foot in the door at Bozell. What finally got me hired wasn't my awful little portfolio. What did it was an interview with McElligott—a sweaty little interrogation I attended wearing my shiny, wide, 1978 tie and where I said "I see" about a hundred times. Tom told me later it was my enthusiasm that convinced him to take a chance on me. That and my promise to put in 80-hour weeks writing the brochures and other scraps that fell off his plate.

Tom hired me as a copywriter in January of '79. He didn't have much work for me during that first month, so he parked me in a conference room with a three-foot stack of books full of the best advertising in the world: the One Show and *Communication Arts* awards annuals. He told me to read them. "Read them all."

He called them "the graduate school of advertising." I think he was right, and I say the same thing to students trying to get into the business today. Get yourself a three-foot stack of your own and read, learn, memorize. Yes, this is a business where we try to break rules, but as T. S. Eliot said, "It's not wise to violate the rules until you know how to observe them."

PORTRAIT OF THE ARTIST
AS A YOUNG HACK

As hard as I studied those awards annuals, most of the work I did that first year wasn't very good. In fact, it stunk. Those early ads of mine were so bad I have to reach for my volume of Edgar Allan Poe to describe them with any accuracy: ". . . a nearly liquid mass of loathsome, detestable putridity."

But don't take my word for it. Here's my very first ad. Just look at Figure 1.4 (for as long as you're able): a dull little ad that doesn't so much revolve around an overused play on the word "interest," as it limps.

Figure 1.4   My first ad. (I know, I know.)

Rumor has it they're still using my first portfolio at poison control centers to induce vomiting. *("Come on now, Jimmy. You ate your sister's antidepressant pills and now you have to look at this bank ad.")*

The point is, if you're like me, you might have a slow beginning. Even my friend Bob Barrie's first ad was terrible. Bob is arguably one of the best art directors in the history of advertising. But his first ad? The boring, flat-footed little headline read: "Win A Boat." We used to give Bob all kinds of grief about that. It became his hallway nickname: "Hey, Win-A-Boat, we're goin' to lunch. You comin'?"

There will come a time when you'll just start to "get it." When you'll no longer waste time traipsing down dead ends or rattling the knobs of doors best left locked. You'll just start to get it. And suddenly, the ads coming out of your office will bear the mark of somebody who knows what the hell he's doing.

Along the way, though, it helps to study how more experienced people have tackled the same problems you'll soon face. On the subject of mentors, Helmut Krone said:

> I asked one of our [young] writers recently, which was more important: Doing your own thing or making the ad as good as it can be? The answer was "Doing my own thing." I disagree violently with that. I'd like to pose a new idea for our age: "Until you've got a better answer, you copy." I copied [famous Doyle Dane art director] Bob Gage for five years.[10]

The question is, who are *you* going to copy while you learn the craft? Whipple? For all the wincing his commercials caused, they worked. A lot of people at Procter & Gamble sent kids through college on Whipple's nickel. And these people can prove it; they have charts and everything.

Bill Bernbach, quoted here,* wasn't big on charts.

> However much we would like advertising to be a science—because life would be simpler that way—the fact is that it is not. It is a subtle, ever-changing art, defying formularization, flowering on freshness and withering on imitation; what was effective one day, for that very

---

*Reprinted with permission from the Oct. 14, 1968, issue of *Advertising Age.* Copyright Crain Communications Inc. 1968.

reason, will not be effective the next, because it has lost the maximum impact of originality.[11]

There is a fork in the road here. You can follow Mr. Bernbach or Mr. Whipple. Mr. Bernbach's path is the one I invite you to come down. It leads to the same place—enduring brands and market leadership—but gets there without costing anybody their dignity. You won't have to apologize to the neighbors for creating that irritating interruption to their sitcom last night. You won't have to explain anything. In fact, the only thing most people will want to know is: "That was so cool. How'd you come up with it?"

This other road has its own rules, if we can call them that. Rules that were first articulated years ago by Mr. Bernbach and his team of pioneers like Bob Levenson, John Noble, Phyllis Robinson, Julian Koenig, and Helmut Krone.

Some may say my allegiance to the famous DDB School will date everything I have to say in this book. Perhaps. Yet a quick glance through their classic Volkswagen ads from the '60s convinces me that the soul of a great advertisement hasn't changed in these years.* Those ads are still great. Intelligent. Clean. Witty. Beautiful. And human.

So with a tip of my hat to those pioneers of brilliant advertising, I offer the ideas in this book. They are the opinions of one writer, gathered over some 20 years in the business of writing, selling, and producing print, radio, and television commercials. God knows, they aren't rules. As copywriter Ed McCabe once said, "I have no use for rules. They only rule out the brilliant exception."

---

*Perhaps the best collection of VW advertisements is a small book edited by the famous copywriter David Abbott: *Remember Those Great Volkswagen Ads?* Holland: European Illustration, 1982.

Figure 2.1   This ad for my friend Alex Bogusky's agency in Miami makes a good point. A smart strategy can take the same message and make it work better.

2

A Sharp Pencil Works Best

Some thoughts on getting started

IS THIS A GREAT JOB OR WHAT?

As an employee in an agency creative department, you will spend most of your time with your feet up on a desk working on an ad. Across the desk, also with his feet up, will be your partner—in my case, an art director. And he will want to talk about movies.

In fact, if the truth be known, you will spend fully one-fourth of your career with your feet up talking about movies.

The ad is due in two days. The media space has been bought and paid for. The pressure's building. And your muse is sleeping off a drunk behind a dumpster somewhere. Your pen lies useless. So you talk movies.

That's when the traffic person comes by. Traffic people stay on top of a job as it moves through the agency. Which means they also stay on top of you. They'll come by to remind you of the horrid things that happen to snail-assed creative people who don't come through with the goods on time.

So you try to get your pen moving. And you begin to work. And working, in this business, means staring at your partner's shoes.

That's what I've been doing from 9 to 5 for almost 20 years. Staring at the bottom of the disgusting tennis shoes on the feet of my partner, parked on the desk across from *my* disgusting tennis shoes. This is the sum and substance of life at an agency.

In movies, they almost never capture this simple, dull, workaday reality of life as a creative person. Don't get me wrong, it's not an easy job. In fact, some days it's almost painful coming up with good ideas. As author Red Smith said, "There's nothing to writing. All you do is sit down at a typewriter and open a vein."[1] But the way movies show it, creative people solve complicated marketing problems between wisecracks and office affairs.

Hollywood's agencies are always "nutty, kooky" sorts of places where odd things are nailed to or stuck on the walls, where weirdly dressed creative people lurch through the hallways metabolizing last night's chemicals, and the occasional goat wanders through in the background.

But that isn't what agencies are like. At least not the four or five agencies where I've worked. Again, don't get me wrong. An ad agency is not a bank. It's not an insurance company. There is a certain amount of joie de vivre in an agency's atmosphere.

Which isn't surprising. Here you have a tight-knit group of young people, many of them making significant salaries just for sitting around with their feet up, solving marketing problems. And talking about movies.

It's a great job because you'll never get bored. One week you'll be knee-deep in the complexities of the financial business, selling market-indexed annuities. The next, you're touring a dog food factory asking about the difference between a "kibble" and a "bit." You'll learn about the business *of* business by studying the operations of hundreds of different kinds of enterprises.

The movies and television also portray advertising as a schlocky business—a parasitic lamprey that dangles from the belly of the business beast. A sort of side business that doesn't really manufacture anything in its own right, where it's all flash over substance, and where silver-tongued salesmen pitch snake oil to a bovine public, sandblast their wallets, and make the 5:20 for Long Island.

Ten minutes of work at a real agency should be enough to convince even the most cynical that an agency's involvement in a
client's business is anything but superficial. Every cubicle on every
floor at an agency is occupied by someone intensely involved in
improving the client's day-to-day business; in shepherding its assets
more wisely, sharpening its business focus, widening its market, even
improving the product.

Ten minutes of work at a real agency should be enough to convince a cynic that you can't sell a product to someone who has no
need for it. That you can't sell a product to someone who can't
afford it. And that advertising can't save a bad product.

In ten minutes the cynic will also see there's no back room where
snickering airbrush artists paint images of breasts into ice cubes, no
slush fund to buy hookers for the client's conventions, and no big
table in the conference room where employees have sex during the
office Christmas party. (Scratch that last one.)

Advertising isn't just some mutant offspring of capitalism. It's one
of the main gears in the machinery of a huge economy, responsible
in great part for one of the highest standards of living the world has
ever seen. That Diet Coke you had an hour before you bought this
book? It's just one of about 30,000 success stories of marketer and
agency working together to bring a product, and with it jobs and
industry, to life.

Diet Coke didn't just happen. Coca-Cola didn't simply roll it out
and hope that people would buy it. Done poorly, they could have
cannibalized their flagship brand, Coke. Done poorly, it could have
been just another one of the well-intentioned product start-ups
that fail in six months. It took a lot of work by both Coca-Cola and
its agency, SSCB, to decipher market conditions, position the product, name it, package it, and pull off the whole billion-dollar introduction.

Advertising, like it or not, is a key ingredient in a competitive
economy and has created a stable place for itself in America's business landscape. Advertising is now a mature industry. And for most
companies, a business necessity.

Why most of it stinks remains a mystery.

Carl Ally, founder of one of the great agencies of the '70s, had a
theory: "There's a tiny percentage of all the work that's great and a

tiny percentage that's lousy. But most of the work—well, it's just there. That's no knock on advertising. How many great restaurants are there? Most aren't good or bad, they're just adequate. The fact is, excellence is tough to achieve in any field."[2]

―――――

WHY NOBODY EVER CHOOSES "BRAND X"

There comes a point when you can't talk about movies anymore and you actually have to get some work done.

You are faced with a blank sheet of paper and you must, in a fixed amount of time, fill it with something interesting enough to be remembered by a customer who in the course of a day will see somewhere around 1,600 other ad messages (as of this writing in '97).[3]

You are not writing a novel somebody pays money for. You are not writing a sitcom somebody enjoys watching. You are writing something most people try to avoid. That is the sad, indisputable truth at the bottom of this business. Nobody wants to see what you are about to put down on paper. People not only dislike advertising, they're becoming immune to most of it—like insects building up resistance to DDT.

When people aren't indifferent to advertising, they're angry at it. If you don't believe me, go to the opening night of a big Hollywood movie. When the third commercial comes up on the screen and it's not the movie, those moans you hear won't be audience ecstasy. People don't want to see your stinkin' ad. Your ad is the *comedian* who comes on stage before a Rolling Stones concert. The audience is drunk and they're angry and they came to see the Stones. And now a comedian has the microphone. You had better be great.

So you try to come up with some advertising concepts that can defeat these barriers of indifference and anger. The ideas you try to conjure, however, aren't done in a vacuum. You're working off a strategy—a sentence or two describing the key competitive message your ad must communicate.

In addition to a strategy, you are working with a brand. Unless it's a new one, that brand brings with it all kinds of baggage, some good and some bad. Ad people call it a brand's "equity."

A brand isn't just the name on the box. It isn't the thing in the box, either. A brand is the sum total of all the emotions, thoughts, images, history, possibilities, and gossip that exist in the marketplace about a certain company.

What's remarkable about brands is that in categories where products are essentially all alike, the best-known and most-well-liked brand has the winning card. In *The Want Makers,* Mike Destiny, former group director for England's Allied Breweries was quoted: "The many competitive brands [of beer] are virtually identical in terms of taste, color, and alcohol delivery, and after two or three pints even an expert couldn't tell them apart. So the consumer is literally drinking the advertising, and the advertising is the brand."[4]

Each brand has its own core value, something it stands for. BMW's is performance. Volvo is known for safety. FedEx is fast. When clients stray from these core values, they usually get into trouble.

Perdue Chicken's excursion into selling frozen turkey is a good example. Here's a brand known for freshness, with 20 years of Frank Perdue on the TV touting the virtues of fresh, pink chicken. Suddenly viewers are being sold turkey, and frozen turkey at that. Perdue's frozen turkey is not enjoying great success. When a client abandons its core values, it also leaves its core competencies, departing from what it does best. And the advertising, even when it's well crafted, rings false and dilutes the flagship brand's image.

A brand isn't just a semantic construct, either. The relationship between the brand and its customers has monetary value; it can amount to literally billions of dollars. Brands are assets, and companies rightfully include them on their financial balance sheets. When you're writing for a brand, you're working with a fragile, extraordinarily valuable thing. Not a lightweight job. Its implications are marvelous.

The ad you're about to do may not make the next million for the brand's marketer, nor may it bring them to Chapter 11. Maybe it's just a half-page ad that runs one time. Yet it's an opportunity to sharpen that brand's image, even if just a little bit. It's a little like being handed the Olympic torch. You won't bear this important symbol all the way from Athens. Your job is just to move it a few miles down the road. Without dropping it in the dirt along the way.

———

STARING AT YOUR PARTNER'S SHOES

For me, writing an ad is unnerving.

You sit down with your partner and put your feet up. You read the account executive's strategy, draw a square on a pad of paper and you both stare at the damned thing. You stare at each other's shoes. You look at the square. You give up and go to lunch.

You come back. The empty square is still there.

So you both go through the product brochures and information folders the account team left in your office. Hmmm. You point out to your partner that this bourbon you're working on is manufactured in a little town with a funny name. Your partner looks out the window and says, "Oh." Down the hallway, a phone rings. He points out that the distillers rotate the aging barrels a quarter turn to the left every few months. You go, "Hmmm." You read that moss on trees happens to grow faster on the sides that face a distillery's aging house. That's interesting.

You feel the glimmer of an idea move through you. You poise your pencil over the page. And it all comes out in a flash of creativity. *(Whoa. Someone call 9-1-1. Report a fire on my drawing pad 'cause I am SMOKIN' hot.)* You put your pencil down, smile, and read what you've written. It's complete rubbish. You call it a day and slink out to see a movie.

This process continues for several days, even weeks, and then without warning an idea just shows up at your door one day, all nattied up like a Jehovah's Witness. You don't know where it comes from. It just shows up.

That's how you make ads. Sorry, there's no big secret. That's basically the drill.

A guy named James Webb Young, a copywriter from the '40s, laid out a five-step process of idea generation that holds water today.

1. You gather as much information on the problem as you can. You read, you underline stuff, you ask questions, you visit the factory.

2. You sit down and actively attack the problem.

3. You drop the whole thing and go do something else while your subconscious mind works on the problem.

4. "Eureka!"

5. You figure out how to implement your idea.[5]

Step two is what this book is about. Thinking up ads.

It isn't just aimless blue-skying, either—a mental version of bad modern dance. It's what author Joseph Heller (a former copywriter) calls "a controlled daydream, a directed reverie." It's imagination disciplined by a single-minded business purpose.

So you start to write. Or doodle. (It doesn't matter which. Good copywriters can think visually; good art directors can write.) You just pick up a pencil and begin. All beginnings are humble, but after several days you begin to translate that flat-footed strategy into something interesting.

The final idea may be a visual. It may be a headline. It may be both. It may arrive whole, like Athena arising out of Zeus's head. Or in pieces—a scribble made by the art director last Friday fits beautifully with a headline the writer comes up with over the weekend. Eventually you get to an idea that dramatizes the benefit of your client's product or service. Dramatizes is the key word. You must dramatize it in a unique, provocative, compelling, and memorable way.

And at the center of this thing you come up with must be a promise. The reader must get something out of the deal. Steve Hayden, most famous for penning Apple Computer's "1984" commercial, said, "If you want to be a well-paid copywriter, please your client. If you want to be an award-winning copywriter, please yourself. If you want to be a great copywriter, please your reader."[6]

Here's the hard part. You have to please your reader and you have to do it in a few seconds.

It's as if you're riding down an elevator with your customer. You're going down only 15 floors. So you have only a few seconds to tell him one thing about your product. One thing. And you have to tell it to him in such an interesting way that he thinks about the promise you've made as he leaves the building, waits for the light, and crosses the street. You have to come up with some little *thing* that sticks in the customer's mind.

By "thing," I don't mean gimmick. Anybody can come up with an unrelated gimmick. Used-car dealers are the national experts with their contrived sales events—"The boss went on vacation and our accountant went crazy!" You might capture somebody's attention for a few seconds with a gimmick. But once the ruse is over and the salesman comes out of the closet in his plaid coat, the customer will only resent you.

Bill Bernbach: "I've got a great gimmick. Let's tell the truth."

The best answers always arise out of the problem itself. Out of the product. Out of the realities of the buying situation. Those are the only paints you have to make your picture, but they are all you need. Any shtick you drag into the situation that is not organically part of the product or customer reality will ring false.

You have more than enough to work with, even with a simple advertising problem. You have your client's product with its brand equities and its benefits. You have the competition's product and its weaknesses. You have the price-quality-value math of the two products. And then you have what the customer brings to the situation—pride, greed, vanity, envy, insecurity, and a hundred other human emotions, wants, and needs, one of which your product satisfies.

"YOU'VE GOT TO PLAY THIS GAME WITH FEAR AND ARROGANCE."

That's one of Kevin Costner's better lines from the baseball movie, *Bull Durham.* I've always thought it had an analog in the advertising business.

There has never been a time in my career I have faced the empty page and not been scared. I was scared as a junior-coassistant-copy-cub-intern. And I'm scared today. Who am I to think I can write something that will interest 8 million people?

Then, a day after winning a medal in the One Show (just about the toughest national advertising awards show there is), I feel bullet-proof. For one measly afternoon, I'm an Ad God. The next day I'm back with my feet up on the table, sweating bullets again.

Somewhere between these two places, however, is where you want to be—a balance between a healthy skepticism of your reason for living and a solar confidence in your ability to come up with a fantastic idea every time you sit down to work. Living at either end of the spectrum will debilitate you. In fact, it's probably best to err on the side of fear.

A small, steady pilot light of fear burning in your stomach is part and parcel of the creative process. If you're doing something that's truly new, you're in an area where there are no signposts yet—no up and down, no good or bad. It seems to me, then, that fear is the constant traveling companion of an advertising person who fancies himself on the cutting edge.

You have to believe that you'll finally get a great idea. You will.

And there is nothing quite like the feeling of cracking a difficult advertising problem. What seemed impossible when you sat down to face the empty white square now seems so obvious. It is this very obviousness of a great idea that prompted Polaroid camera inventor E. H. Land to define creativity as "the sudden cessation of stupidity." You look at the idea you've just come up with, slap your forehead, and go, "Of course, it *has* to be this."

The harder the problem is to solve, the more gratifying it is to do it. Look at this great ad for Penn tennis balls, written by my buddy Mike Gibbs (Fig. 2.2). This is the kind of ad I think you should aspire to.

No, it's not a sexy, four-color magazine spread for Tahiti tourism. But it's for a real client. It solves a real advertising problem. And it solves it spectacularly well (on a low budget, to boot).

"GOOD ADVERTISING BUILDS SALES. GREAT ADVERTISING BUILDS FACTORIES."

Solving a difficult advertising problem is a great feeling. Even better is the day, weeks or months later, when an account executive pops his head in your door and says sales are up. It never ceases to amaze me when that happens. Not that I doubt the power of advertising, but it's often hard to follow the thread from the scratchings on my pad all the way to a ringing cash register in Akron, Ohio. Yet it works.

People generally deny advertising has any effect on them. They'll insist they're immune to it. And perhaps, taken on a person-by-

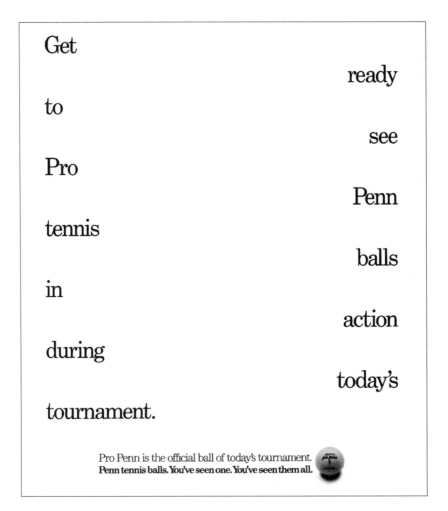

Figure 2.2   The writer told me this job was originally offered to senior creatives at the agency, but they passed on it. It was just a "dumb program ad."

person basis, the effect of your ad is indeed modest. But over time, the results are undeniable. It's been said that advertising is like wind on desert sands. The changes occurring at any given hour on any particular dune are small. But over time, the whole landscape changes.

Try this on: 1980—Absolut Vodka is a little nothing brand. Selling 12,000 cases a year. That's nothing. (I'm sure 6,000 of that was *me*.) Ten years and one campaign later, this colorless, nearly tasteless, and odorless product is the preferred brand, selling nearly 3 million cases a year. All because of the advertising (Fig. 2.3).

More anecdotal, but equally impressive, were the results of the trade campaign created to attract advertisers to the pages of *Rolling Stone* magazine. After Fallon McElligott's famous "Perception/ Reality" campaign was up and running (Fig. 2.4), publisher Jann Wenner was reported as saying, "It was like someone came in with a wheelbarrow of money and dumped it on the floor."

It's a great business, make no mistake. I see what copywriter Tom Monahan meant when he said, "Advertising is the rock 'n' roll of the business world."

"THE QUALITY GOES IN BEFORE THE NAME GOES ON."

Before you put pencil to paper, there is background work to do. You won't be doing it alone, though. You'll have help from the account executives.

Account execs are the people in charge of an account at an agency. They analyze the market, study the competition, and arrange

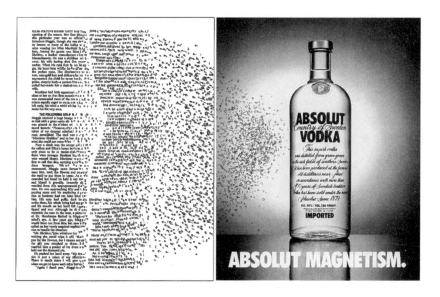

Figure 2.3   A campaign with more legs than the Rockettes.

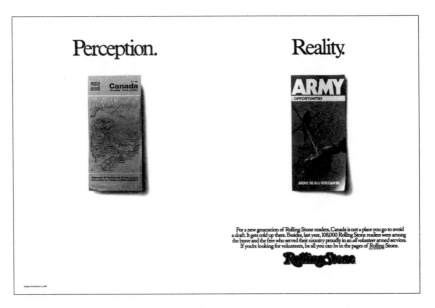

*Figure 2.4   A map of Canada vs. an Army brochure. First scribbled
on a napkin in a New York City diner by writer Bill Miller,
this campaign for* Rolling Stone *magazine went on to be named
one of the ten best campaigns of the 1980s.*

for and interpret the research. They formulate strategy, set budgets, and do a whole bunch of other stuff, some of it boring. They also help you present work to the client. Overall, they're the liaison between client and agency, explaining one to the other.

Some AEs are great, some so-so, and some bad. It will pay to hitch up with the smart ones as soon as you can. The good ones have the soul of a creative person and will share your excitement over a great ad. They're articulate, honest, inspiring, and have a better batting average selling your work.

Here are some things I've learned from the great account people I've worked with.

Get to know your client's business as well as you can.

Bill Bernbach said, "The magic is in the product. . . . You've got to live with your product. You've got to get steeped in it. You've got to get saturated with it."

The moral for writers and art directors is: Do the factory tour. I'm serious. Go if you get the chance. Ask a million questions. How is the product made? What ingredients does it have? What are the quality control criteria? Read every brochure. Read every memo you can get your hands on. You may find ideas waiting in the middle of a spec sheet ready to be transplanted kit and caboodle into an ad. Learn the company's business.

Your clients are going to trust you more if you can talk to them about their industry in *their* terms. They'll quickly find you boring or irrelevant if all you can speak about with authority is Century Italic. Your grasp of the client's marketing situation has to be as well versed as any account executive's. There are no shortcuts. Know the client. Know their product. Know their market. It will pay off.

Louis Pasteur said, "Chance favors the prepared mind."

On the other hand, there is value in staying stupid.

This dissenting opinion was brought to my attention by a great copy-writer, Mark Fenske. Mark says, "Don't *ever* give into the temptation to take the factory tour. Resist. It makes you think like the client. What happens is you'll start to come up with the same answers the client does."

Mark thinks, as many do, that keeping your "tabula" extremely "rasa" makes your thinking fresher. He may be right. There's also this to consider: When you're on the factory floor watching the caps get put on the bottles, you are a long way from the customer's reality. All the customer cares about is "What's in it for me?"

Get to know the client's customers as well as you can.

There is a relatively new discipline in this business called "planning."

It is the job of account planners to learn as much as they can about the client's customers and feed it back to both client and agency. Read everything your planners give you before putting pen to paper. Remember, most of the ads you do will be targeted to people outside your small social circle, people with whom you have no more in common than U.S. citizenship.

Take farming. I've written TV commercials selling herbicides to soybean farmers, but what do I know about farming? As a kid, I couldn't even keep an *ant farm* alive a week after it arrived in the mail. Getting into the mind-set of a soybean farmer took plenty of work, mostly reading. Your account planners can give you piles of material to study.

But don't just read it. Feel it. Take a deep breath and sink slowly into the world of the person you're writing to. Maybe you're selling a retirement community. You're talking to older people. People living on fixed incomes. Maybe they're worried about the nest egg running out. It hurts when they get out of a chair. The idea of shoveling snow has dark-red cardiac overtones. How does it *feel* to be them?

Be in the original meeting where the strategy is formed.

If there's any flabby thinking in that first strategy meeting, it will be impossible to do a good ad. Garbage in, garbage out. So be in the original meeting. It's not always possible and you probably can't do it for every ad that comes along. But for those big projects, it pays to be there for the early thinking on strategy.

Examine the current positioning of your product.

There's a book called *Positioning: The Battle for Your Mind,* one I recommend with many caveats. (Though the strategic thinking of the authors is sound, I have many differences with them on the subject of creativity, which they declare irrelevant.)

The authors, Reis and Trout, maintain that the customer's head has a finite amount of space to remember products. In each category, there's room for perhaps three brand names. If your product isn't in one of those slots, you must "de-position" a competitor to take its place. For example, in 7-Up's campaign from the early '70s, instead of positioning it as a clear soft drink with a lemon-lime flavor, 7-Up took on the big three brown colas by positioning itself as "The Un-cola."

Before you start, look at the current positioning of your product. What positions do the competitors occupy? What niches are undefended? Should you concentrate on defining your client's position, or do some de-positioning of the competition?

If you can, try to claim the high ground. In every product category, there's usually one adjective every company wants, one benefit more important than any other. In bread, it can be freshness. In tissues, it can be softness. (Hence Mr. Whipple.) Plant your flag on the highest mountain you can.

Insist on a tight strategy.

Creative director Norman Berry wrote: "English strategies are very tight, very precise. Satisfy the strategy and the idea cannot be faulted even though it may appear outrageous. Many . . . strategies are often too vague, too open to interpretation. 'The strategy for this product is taste,' they'll say. But that is not a strategy. Vague strategies inhibit. Precise strategies *liberate.*"[7]

You need a tight strategy.

On the other hand, a strategy can become too tight. When there's no play in the wheel, an overly specific strategy demands a very narrow range of executions and becomes by proxy an execution itself. Good AEs and planners can fine-tune a strategy by moving it up and down a continuum between broad, meaningless statements and little pursed-lipped creative dictums masquerading as strategies.

Ultimately, a good strategy is inspiring. You can pull a hundred rabbits out of the same hat, creating wildly different executions that are all on strategy. Goodby, Silverstein & Partners' magnificent "milk deprivation" strategy called forth a long string of wonderful "Got Milk?" executions.*

The final strategy must yield good advertising.

Sometimes a strategy can look good on paper and bad on a layout pad. Usually, you won't discover this until you've worked on it awhile.

Field Marshal Erwin Rommel wrote, "The best strategic plan is useless if it cannot be executed tactically." So, if it's not working, go back to the account executives and present your beginning ideas, lame as they may be. Explain that the agreed-upon strategy may sound right, but it leads to ads that don't. Then sit down and hash out a new strategy with the same or a similar message, but one that allows you to express it with simplicity and power.

---

*See *Communication Arts,* December 1995, for examples.

The final strategy should be simple.

Advertising isn't brain surgery.

People live and think in broad strokes. Ask some guy in a mall about cars. He'll tell you Volvos are safe, Porsches are fast, and Jeeps are rugged. Boom. Where's the rocket science here? There isn't any.

You want people who feel X about your product to feel Y. That's about it. We're talking one adjective here. Most of the time, we're talking about going into a customer's brain and tacking one adjective onto a client's brand. That's all. DeWalt tools are tough. Apple computers are easy to use.

I'm reminded of how Steven Spielberg said he preferred movie ideas that could be summed up in a sentence. "Lost alien befriends lonely boy to get home."

The moral is, keep it simple. Don't let the account executives or the client make you overthink it. Try not to slice too thin. Think in bright colors.

Make sure what you have to say matters.

It must be relevant. It must matter to somebody, somewhere. It has to offer something customers want or solve a problem they have, whether it's a car that won't start or a drip that won't stop.

If you don't have something relevant to say, tell your clients to put their wallets away. Because no matter how well you execute it, an unimportant message has no receiver. The tree falls in the forest.

Testing strategy is better than testing executions.

This is the best of all possible worlds, and the day hell freezes over, all clients will be testing this way. A few do this now. Here's how it works.

You sit down with the client, the planners, and the account team. You explore all the possible strategies available to your brand. You settle on five or six—ten, if you want.

Then you make what are called "benefit boards." Simple, flat-footed layout things that look and feel like ads, but aren't.

For example, say the client manufactures aspirin. The pictures could be anything really—a shot of a person nursing a headache or a close-up of two aspirins on a tabletop. Next to the picture on each board is a headline pitching a different angle on the product:

"Faster-acting Throbinex." "Throbinex is easy on the stomach." "Smaller, easier-to-swallow pills." Just crank them out. These aren't ads. They're benefits.

Show ten different boards like these to a focus group and you'll come away with a good idea of which messages resonate with customers. It's a great place to start. In fact, it's the only place to start.

Go to the focus groups.

I used to hate doing this. I still do. I think pretesting concepts by showing rough layouts and storyboards to customers is a bane on the industry. (But more on that later, in Chapter 9.)

For now, I say go to the groups, if only for the selfish reason that it helps you sell work to the client. Because once you've put in the hours at the groups, you can say, "Yes, I sat there and stared through the glass at those people. I think I have a good idea of which strategies will work, what customers like and what they don't, and in my opinion this campaign will work."

Read the publications your ads will be in.

Check out the articles. See what your target customer is reading. Case the joint. Get a feel for the place your ad will be appearing.

Read the awards books.

Take a little inspiration from the excellence you see there. Then get ready to do something just as great. The best awards books are from the One Show and *Communication Arts,* as well as the British D&AD annuals.

Look at the competitor's advertising.

Each category quickly manages to establish its own brand of boring. Learn the visual clichés. Creep through the woods, part the branches, and study the ground your competitors occupy. What is their strategy? What is their look? Those schmucks. They don't know what's coming.

Now comes the fun part. Sharpening your pencil and sitting down to make a great ad.

Figure 3.1   A short five-word course in advertising.

3

A Clean Sheet of Paper
Making an ad—the broad strokes

LET'S BEGIN THIS PART OF OUR DISCUSSION with a quotation from Helmut Krone, the man who did what I think is the industry's first good ad (Fig. 1.2): "I start with a blank piece of paper and try to fill it with something interesting." So that's what I do, if I'm working on a print ad. I get a clean sheet of paper and draw a small rectangle. I figure if an idea doesn't work in a small space, it's not going to work.

And then I start.

SAYING THE RIGHT THING THE RIGHT WAY

Remember, you have two problems to solve: the client's and yours.

You solve the account team's problem by saying exactly the right thing. That's relatively easy. It's the strategy. Your problem is solved by saying it well. You aren't done until both problems are solved.

Bernbach warned, "Dullness won't sell your product, but neither will irrelevant brilliance."

My friend, Pat Fallon, addressed the dichotomy this way:* "In the very best advertising there is no difference, no discernible distinction between strategy and execution. The 'creative' idea is the best, most effective and elegant statement of the proper strategy."[1]

The moral? Do both perfectly.

Pose the problem as a question.

Creativity in advertising is problem solving. When you state the problem as a bald question, sometimes the answers suggest themselves. Take care not to simply restate the problem in the terms it was brought to you; you're not likely to discover any new angles that way. Pose the question again and again, from entirely different perspectives.

"What would make a person pay twice as much for a bottle of whiskey just because it's manufactured in small batches? . . . What is the main difference between the manufacturing process of large and small distilleries? . . . If it takes just as long to age a lot of whiskey as it does a little, why bother with small numbers?"

As philosopher John Dewey put it: "A problem well-stated is a problem half-solved." It can work. Eric Clark reminds us just how it works in his book, *The Want Makers.*

> In the 1960s, a team wrestled for weeks for an idea to illustrate the reliability of the Volkswagen in winter. Eventually they agreed that a snowplow driver would make an excellent spokesman. The breakthrough came a week later when one of the team wondered aloud, "How does the snowplow driver *get* to his snowplow?"[2]

If you've never seen it, the VW "snowplow" commercial is vintage Doyle Dane. A man gets in his Volkswagen and drives off through deep snow into a blizzard. At the end, we see where he's driving: the garage where the county snowplows are parked. The voice-over then asks, "Have you ever wondered how the man who drives a

---

*Reprinted with permission from the August 7, 1989, issue of *Advertising Age.* Copyright, Crain Communications Inc. 1989.

snowplow...drives *to* the snowplow? This one drives a Volkswagen. So you can stop wondering."

Don't be afraid to ask dumb questions.

That blank slate we sometimes bring to a problem-solving session can work in our favor. We ask the obvious questions that people too close to the problem often forget. In the question's very naïveté we sometimes find simple answers that have been overlooked.

Ask yourself what would make *you* want to buy the product.

A simple enough piece of advice and one I often forget about while I'm busy trying to write an ad. Sit across from yourself at your desk. Quiet your mind. And ask.

Then try the flip side: What would you do if you were the one bankrolling the campaign?

There was a writer at my agency who was also an investor in a new product—some kind of running gear. He was both the writer and the client. When he sat down to do ads for a company whose failure would cost him a significant amount of money, he saw how some of the things he hated hearing from clients had merit.

Copywriter John Matthews wrote, "You learn a lot more about poker when you play for money and not for matchsticks."

Find the central truth about your product.

Find the central truth about your whole product category. The central *human* truth. Hair coloring isn't about looking younger. It's about self-esteem. Cameras aren't about pictures. They're about stopping time and holding life as the sands run out.

There are ads to be written all around the edges of any product. But get to the ones written right from the *essence* of the thing.

Reprinted here is an ad by my friend, Dean Buckhorn, for the American Floral Marketing Council (Fig. 3.2). He could have done something about how "purdy" flowers are. He didn't and instead focused on one of the central human truths about this category—the use of flowers as a ticket out of the "Casa di Canine."

Figure 3.2   The headline could have been something boring like:
"We're proud of our wide variety of beautiful flower arrangements.
One's just right for your budget."

Try the competitor's product.

What's wrong with it? More important, what do you like about it? What's good about their advertising?

Then try this trick. In *Marketing Warfare,* Reis and Trout suggested, "Find a weakness in the leader's strength and attack at that point."[3]

A good example comes to mind, again from the pens of Bernbach's crew. Avis Rent A Car was only No. 2. So Avis suggested you come to them instead of Hertz because "The line at our counter is shorter."

Dramatize the benefit.

Not the features of the product, but the benefit those features provide the user, or what some call "the benefit of the benefit." There is an old advertising maxim that expresses this wisdom in a way that's hard to improve: "People don't buy quarter-inch drill bits. They buy quarter-inch holes."

Avoid style; focus on substance.

Remember, styles change; typefaces and design and art direction, they all change. Fads come and go. But people are always people.

They want to look better, to make more money; they want to feel better, to be healthy. They want security, attention, and achievement. These things about people aren't likely to change. So focus your efforts on speaking to these basic needs rather than tinkering with the current visual affectations. Focus first on the substance of what you want to say. Then worry about how.

Make the claim in your ad something that is incontestable.

Make it something that can't be argued about. Facts can't be refuted. There are some products where this advice won't apply. Products that are all image. Or products with no real difference worth hanging your hat on, like, say, paper clips.

But when you have a fact at your command, use it. When you can say, "This product lasts 20 years," what's to argue with? State fact, not manufactured nonsense about, oh, say, how "We Put the 'Qua' in Quality."

GET SOMETHING, ANYTHING, ON PAPER.

The artist Nathan Olivera wrote, "All art is a series of recoveries from the first line. The hardest thing to do is put down the first line. But you must."

Here are some ideas to help you get started.

First, say it straight. Then say it great.

To get the words flowing, sometimes it helps to simply write out what you want to say. Make it memorable, different, or new later. First, just say it.

Try this. Begin your headline with: "This is an ad about . . ." And then keep writing. Who knows? You might find by the time you get to the end of a sentence, you have something just by snipping off the "This is an ad about" part. Even if you don't, you've focused. A good first step.

Whatever you do, just start writing. Don't let the empty page (what Hemingway called "the white bull") intimidate you. Bill Westbrook once showed me a letter written to him by none other than E. B. White. Bill had asked the famous author for advice on how to get past a bad case of writer's block.

White's answer: "Just say the words."

Restate the strategy and put some spin on it.

Think of the strategy statement as a lump of clay. You've got to sculpt it into something interesting to look at. So begin by taking the strategy and saying it some other way, any way. Say it faster. Say it in English. Then in slang. Shorten it. Punch it up. Try anything that will change the strategy statement from something you'd overhear in an elevator at a sales convention to a message you'd see spray-painted on an alley wall.

Club Med's tag line could have been "A Great Way to Get Away." It could have been "More than Just a Beach." Fortunately, Ammirati & Puris had the account and it became: "Club Med. The Antidote for Civilization."

Be careful, too, not to let your strategy show. Many ads suffer from this transparence, and it happens when you fail to put enough creative spin on the strategy. Your ad remains flat and obvious, there's no magic to it, and reading it is a bit of a letdown. It's like Dorothy discovering the Wizard of Oz is just some knucklehead behind a curtain.

Allow yourself to come up with terrible ideas.

In *Bird by Bird,* her book on the art of writing fiction, Anne Lamott says:

> The only way I can get anything written at all is to write really, really crappy first drafts. That first draft is the child's draft, where you let it pour out and then let it romp all over the place, knowing that no one is going to see it and that you can shape it later. You just let this child-like part of you channel whatever voices and visions come through and onto the page. If one of the characters wants to say, "Well, so what, Mr. Poopy Pants?," you let her.[4]

Same thing in advertising. Start with "Free to qualified customers" and go from there.

Remember, notebook paper is not made solely for recording gems of transcendent perfection. A sheet of paper costs about one-squillionth of a cent. It isn't a museum frame. It's a workbench. Write. Keep writing. Don't stop.

Allow your partner to come up with terrible ideas.

The quickest way to shut down your partner's contribution to the creative process is to roll your eyes at a bad idea. Don't. Even if the idea truly and most sincerely blows, just say, "That's interesting," scribble it down and move on.

Feed a baby idea lots of milk and burp it regularly.

Nurture a newly hatched idea. Until it grows up, you don't know what it's going to be. So don't look for what's wrong with a new idea, look for what's right. And no playing the devil's advocate just yet. Instead, do what writer Sydney Shore suggests: Play the "angel's advocate." Coax the thing along.

Share all your ideas with your partner, even the half-formed ones.

Just because an idea doesn't work yet, it might. I sometimes find I get something that looks like it might go somewhere, but I can't do anything with it. It just sits there. Some wall inside prevents me from taking it to the next level. That's when my partner scoops up my miserable little half idea and runs with it over the goal line.

Remember, the point of teamwork isn't to impress your partner by sliding a fully finished idea across the conference-room table. It's about how $1 + 1 = 3$.

Spend some time away from your partner, thinking on your own.

I know many teams who actually prefer to start that way. It gives you both a chance to look at the problem from your own perspective before you bring your ideas to the table.

Let your subconscious mind do it.

Where do ideas come from? I have no earthly idea. Around 1900, a writer named Charles Haanel said true creativity comes from "a benevolent stranger, working on our behalf." Novelist Isaac Singer said, "There are powers who take care of you, who send you patience and stories." And film director Joe Pytka said, "Good ideas come from God." I think they're probably all correct. It's not so much *our* coming up with great ideas as it is creating a canvas where a painting can appear.

So do what Marshall Cook suggests in his book *Freeing Your Creativity:* "Creativity means getting out of the way. . . . If you can quiet the yammering of the conscious, controlling ego, you can begin to hear your deeper, truer voice in your writing. . . . [not the] noisy little you that sits out front at the receptionist's desk and tries to take credit for everything that happens in the building."[5]

Stop the chatter in your head. Go into Heller's "controlled daydream." Breathe from your stomach. If you're lucky, sometimes the ideas just begin to appear. What does the *ad* want to say? Not you, the ad. Shut up. Listen.

Try writing down words from the product's category.

You're selling outboard engines? Start a list on the side of the page: Fish. Water. Pelicans. Flotsam. Jetsam. Atlantic. Titanic. Ishmael.

What do these words make you think of? Pick up two of them and put them together like Tinkertoys. You have to start somewhere. Sure, it sounds stupid. The whole creative *process* is stupid.

It's like washing a pig. It's messy, it has no rules, no clear beginning, middle, or end; it's kind of a pain in the ass, and when you're done, you're not sure if the pig is clean or even why you were washing a pig in the first place. Welcome to the creative department.

Stare at a picture that has the emotion of the ad you want to do.

Have you ever tried to write an angry letter when you weren't angry? Oh, you manage to get a few cuss words on paper, but there's no fire to it. The same can be said for writing a good ad. You need to be in the mood.

I once had to do some ads for a new magazine called *Family Life*. The editors said this wasn't going to be just another of those "baby magazines," which are very much like diapers—soft, fluffy, and full of . . . My point is, they wanted ads that captured the righteous emotion of the editorial. Raising a child is the most moving, most important thing you'll ever do.

To get in the mood, I did two things. I reread a wonderful book by Anna Quindlen on the joys and insanities of parenting called *Living Out Loud*. I'd soak up a couple of pages before I sat down to write. When I was ready to put pen to paper, I propped up a number of different stock photos of children, including a picture of a child in a raincoat, sitting in a puddle. (See Fig. 3.3.)

As you can see in the ad reprinted here, the idea didn't come directly out of the photo, but in a way it did. It's worked for me. You might want to try it.

Find a villain.

Find a bad guy you can beat up in the stairwell. Every client has an enemy, particularly in mature categories where growth has to come out of somebody else's hide.

Figure 3.3   The headline was inspired by the photograph.
The copy reads: "The years from age 3 to 12 go by so fast.
Only one magazine makes the most of them."

Your enemy can be the other guy's scummy, overpriced product. It can also be some pain or inconvenience the client's product spares you. If the product's a toothpaste, the villain can be tooth decay, the dentist, the drill, or that little pointy thing Laurence Olivier used on Dustin Hoffman in *Marathon Man*. ("Is it *safe?*") A villain can come from another product category altogether, in the form of what's called an "indirect competitor." Parker pens, for example, could be said to have an indirect competitor in word processors.

A knee gracefully raised to a villain's groin isn't just fun, it's profitable. Because competitive positioning is implicit in every villain paradigm.

It's also an easy and fun place from which to write. Mom was always telling us about "constructive criticism." Yeah, well, highly underrated and much more fun is the concept of "destructive criticism."

Mom never quoted Genghis Khan to us either, but a line from the famous village-burner seems appropriate here: "The greatest joy a man can know is to conquer his enemies and drive them before him. To ride his horses and take away his possessions."

See, advertising is fun.

"Tell the truth and run."

This old Yugoslavian proverb is a reminder of the power of truth. Even if you have an unpleasant truth, say it.

"We're Avis. We're only No. 2. So we try harder." Totally believable. More important, I *like* a company that would say this about themselves. America loves an underdog.

Perhaps the biggest underdog of all time was Volkswagen. VW was the king of self-deprecation. The honest voice Doyle Dane Bernbach created for this odd-looking little car turned its weaknesses into strengths. This ad is a perfect example (Fig. 3.4).

Does the medium lend itself to your message?

Some great ads have been done playing off of the very place they appear. This is well-tilled ground, so take care that your idea hasn't been done 200 times before. But when it works, it works.

The ad from Australia's Taronga Zoo (Fig. 3.5) is a great example, reprinted at actual size.

Figure 3.4 Many other clients would've urged the agency to avoid, hide, or deny the small size of their car. Not VW.

Be provocative.

Sometimes the best way to bring the message home is to gallop into town and splash mud all over decent citizens.

Provocative is good. It gets your client talked about. The famous Wonderbra campaign is a good example. The visual: a photo of a drop-dead gorgeous model answering the front door wearing a push-up bra. Some of the headlines: "You're early." Or "Newton was wrong." And "Hello Boys." Go over the line once in a while, when it seems right. Just a couple of steps. Going way over the line may backfire on you. And please, don't take this as permission to do a "pee-pee" joke. If I see even one more ad with a sly reference to penises, I think I shall retire to my chambers, close the door, and gently weep.

Remember, being provocative just because you *can* isn't the point. Like Bernbach said, "Be sure your provocativeness stems from your product." This ad I did for People for the Ethical Treatment of Animals qualifies (Fig. 3.6). When you have a client like this, especially a public service client with a $7 media budget, it's time to take out all the stops. Go for broke.

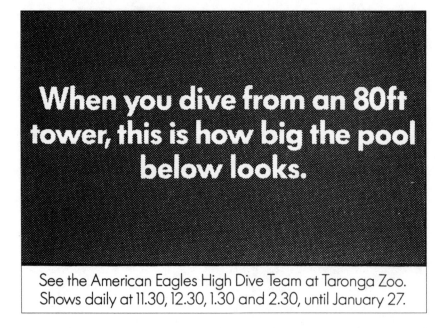

Figure 3.5   *Spinning your concept off the shape or placement of the ad is fun. But be careful. This is well-tilled ground.*

Figure 3.6   Being provocative is good. It's easy, too, when you have a great pro bono client like People for the Ethical Treatment of Animals.

"DO I HAVE TO DRAW YOU A PICTURE?"

Be visual and go short on the copy.

The screensaver on the computers at London's Bartle Bogle Hegarty reads, "Words are a barrier to communication." Creative director (CD) John Hegarty says, "I just don't think people read ads."

I don't think most people read ads either, at least not the body copy. There's a reason they say a picture is worth a thousand words. When you first picked up this book, what did you look at? I'm betting it was the pictures.

Granted, if you interest readers with a good visual or headline, yes, they may go on to read your copy. But the point is, you should try to solve the problem visually if you can. As the larger brands become globally marketed, visual solutions will become even more important. Visuals translate better than words.

Visual solutions are so universal, they work even after years in a deep freeze. Look at this 1879 ad for the Diebold Safe & Lock Company of Cleveland, Ohio (Fig. 3.7). Putting aside the issue of whether this is a good ad or not, I'll bet it's a lot better than any verbal equivalent from other safe manufacturers of the times. ("Doers of Evil and Kriminal Minds agree, Monies safekept in an Acme Vault are ne'er Pilfered For Gambling & Likker.")

The ad for Mitsubishi's Space Wagon (in Fig. 3.8) from Singapore's Ball Partnership is one of my all-time favorites. The message is delivered entirely with one picture and a thimbleful of words. What could you possibly add to or take away from this concept?

Relying on one simple visual means it assumes added responsibilities and a bigger job description. You can't bury your main selling idea in the copy. If the reader doesn't get what you're trying to say from the visual, he won't get it. The page is turned.

Don't take my word for it. Watch someone in the airport read a magazine. They whip through, usually backwards, at about two seconds per page. They glance at the clock on the wall. They turn a page. They think about the desperate, pimpled loneliness of their high school years. They look at a page. They see your ad.

Figure 3.7   Whether this visual ad from 1879 is good is debatable.
Whether it still works fast is not.

*Figure 3.8   Long-copy ads can be great. I happen to prefer visual solutions.
I think they work faster.*

If you can get them to take in your visual (or read your headline), your ad is a *resounding* success. Break out the Champale. Call your parents. You are a genius.

Coax an interesting visual out of your product.

My little boy, Reed, and I went through this mental exercise one day using a toy car. I held the car in its traditional four-wheels-to-the-ground position and asked him, "What's this?" "A car," he said. I tipped it on its side. Two wheels on the ground made the image "a motorcycle." I tipped the car on its curved top. He saw a hull and said, "Boat." When I set it tailpipe to ground pointing straight up, he saw propulsion headed moonward and told me, "It's a rocket."

Look at your product and do the same thing. Visualize it on its side. Upside down. Make its image rubber. Stretch your product visually six ways to Sunday, marrying it with other visuals, other icons, and see what you get—always keeping in mind you're trying to coax out of the product a dramatic image with a selling benefit.

What if it were bigger? Smaller? On fire? What if you gave it legs? Or a brain? What if you put a door in it? What is the wrong way to use it? How else could you use it? What other thing does it look like? What could you substitute for it? Take your product, change it visually, and by doing so, dramatize a customer benefit.

Get the visual clichés out of your system right away.

Certain visuals are just old. Somewhere out there is a Home for Tired Old Visuals. Sitting there in rocking chairs on the porch are visuals like Uncle Sam, a devil with a pitchfork, and a proud lion, just rocking back and forth waiting for someone to use them in an ad once again. And grousing, "When we were young, we were in all kinds of ads. People used to *love* us."

It's good to pay a short visit to the icons at the Home for Tired Old Visuals. Tell them you really liked their stuff when you first saw them in 1984. And when you saw them again in 1985. (*"Loved you in '86. You still had it in '87, baby."*) They will nod off after awhile. This is when you sneak away, never to return.

Show, don't tell.

Telling a reader why your product has merit is never as powerful as showing him. I could take all day explaining how well a certain brand of vacuum cleaner works, but you'll sit up and take notice when I plug it in and show how it empties a sandbox in under a minute and can still suck the spots off a dalmatian.

Showing the benefit of your product also allows readers to reach their own conclusions. It's more involving.

This great ad by BMP in London for Fisher-Price's anti-slip roller skates (Fig. 3.9) is a good example of the benefits of showing your story, not telling it. It's one of my all-time favorites.

Saying isn't the same as being.

This is a corollary to the previous point. If a client says, "I want people to think our company is cool," the answer isn't an ad saying, "We're cool." The answer is to *be* cool. Nike never once said, "Hey, we're cool." They just were.

As Miss Manners politely points out, "It is far more impressive when others discover your good qualities without your help."

Figure 3.9 The mental image this ad paints of two kids landing on their duffs is more powerful than actually showing them that way.

"THE REVERSE SIDE ALSO HAS A REVERSE SIDE."

When everybody else is zigging, you should zag.

I am required by law to trot out this tired old advertising cliché. Yes, it's true. And there, I've said it.

Steve Dunn, a fabulous art director from London, put it this way: "One thing I recommend is at some point you should turn everything on its head. Logos usually go lower right, so put them top left. Product shots are usually small, make them big. Instead of headlines being more prominent than the body copy, do the opposite. It's perverse, but I'm constantly surprised how many times it works."[6]

Don't be different just to be different.

You must have a reason to zag, one beyond just the desire to be different. Bill Bernbach said it best:

> Be provocative. But be sure your provocativeness stems from your product. You are not right if in your ad you stand a man on his head

just to get attention. You are right if [it's done to] show how your product keeps things from falling out of his pockets.

Merely to let your imagination run riot, to dream unrelated dreams, to indulge in graphic acrobatics is not being creative. The creative person has harnessed his imagination. He has disciplined it so that every thought, every idea, every word he puts down, every line he draws . . . makes more vivid, more believable, more persuasive the . . . product advantage.[7]

Consider the opposite of your product.

What doesn't the product do? Who doesn't need the product? When is the product a waste of money? Study the inverse problem and see where negative thinking leads.

I saw a great opposite idea in a student book. It was a small poster for a paint manufacturer that painters could put up after their job was finished. Above the company's logo, this warning—"Dry Paint."

Move back and forth between wide-open, blue-sky thinking and critical analysis.

It's like this: Up in my brain, there's this poet guy. Smokes a lot. Wears black. He's *so* creative. And "chicks dig 'im." He's got a million ideas. But 999,000 of them suck. He knows this because there's also a certified public accountant up there who tells him so.

"That won't work. You *suck*."

The CPA is a no-nonsense guy who clips coupons and knows how to fix the car when the poet runs it into the ditch on his way to "Beret World." Between the two of them though, I manage to come up with a few ideas that actually work.

The trick is to give each one his say. Let the poet go first. Be loose. Be wild. Then let the CPA come in, take measurements, and see what actually works. I sense that I'm about to run this metaphor into the ground, so I'll just bow out here by saying, go back and forth between wild dorm-room creativity and critical dad's-basement analysis, always keeping your strategy statement in mind.

Interpret the problem using different mental processes.

See what happens. From a book called *Conceptual Blockbusting* by James Adams, I excerpt this list[8]:

build up	dissect	transpose
eliminate	symbolize	unify
work forward	simulate	distort
work backward	manipulate	rotate
associate	transform	flatten
generalize	adapt	squeeze
compare	substitute	stretch
focus	combine	abstract
purge	separate	translate
verbalize	vary	expand
visualize	repeat	reduce
hypothesize	multiply	exaggerate
define	invert	understate

Put on different thinking caps.

How would the folks at today's top agencies solve your problem? Chiat/Day, for instance. How would they solve it at Wieden & Kennedy? At Goodby? How would they approach your problem at Disney? At Microsoft? At Amblin?

Shake the Etch-A-Sketch in your head, start over constantly, and come at the problem from wildly different angles. Don't keep sniffing all four sides of the same fire hydrant. Run through the entire neighborhood.

Metaphors must've been invented for advertising.

They aren't always right for the job, but when they are they can be a quick and powerful way to communicate. Shakespeare did it: "Shall I compare thee to a summer's day?"

In my opinion (and the neo-Freudian, Carl Jung's), the mind works and moves through and thinks in and dreams in symbols. Red means ANGER. A dog means LOYAL. A hand coming out of water means

HELP. Ad people might say that each of these images has an "equity," something they *mean* by dint of the associations people have ascribed to them over the years. You may be able to use these equities to your client's advantage, particularly when the product or service is intangible like, say, insurance. A metaphor can help make it real.

What makes metaphors particularly useful to your craft is they're a sort of conceptual shorthand and say with one image what you may otherwise need 20 words to say. They get a lot of work done quickly and simply.

The trick is doing it well. Just picking up an image/symbol and plopping it down next to your client's logo won't work. But when you can take an established image, put some spin on it, and use it in some new and unexpected way that relates to your product advantage, things can get pretty cool.

As soon as I put those words on paper, I remembered a marvelous British campaign for a business weekly. In the one reprinted here (Fig. 3.10), an unadorned keyhole is simply plopped down next to the logo. One stroke is all it takes to give the impression *The Economist* has inside information on corporations. So much for my rules.

Still, I stand by my advice. Symbols lifted right off the rack usually won't fit your communication needs and typically need some spin put on them.

Figure 3.10   Metaphor as ad. Keyhole = competitive business information.

Example: I had a client, Barnett Banks, who wanted to tell realtors they offered quick approval on mortgage loans. It seemed to me and the art director, Diane Cook-Tench, that a cross section of a tree trunk with its concentric rings was a great way to show the slow passage of time. The spin we put on that metaphor was two little call outs, or captions: one pointing to the center ring saying, "Date of mortgage application" and one pointing to the final outer ring, "Date of mortgage approval." (See Fig. 3.11.)

Verbal metaphors can work equally well. I remember a great ad from Nike touting their athleticwear for baseball. Below the picture of a man at bat, the headline read, "Proper attire for a curveball's funeral."

"Wit invites participation."

Part of what makes metaphors in ads so effective is that they involve the reader. They use images already in the reader's mind, twist them to our message's purpose, and ask the reader to close the loop for us. There are other ways you can leave some work to the reader, and when you do it correctly, you usually have a better ad.

Here's an example. Nikon cameras ran an ad with the headline: "If you can picture it in your head, it was probably taken with a Nikon." Above this headline were four solid black squares, and inside each square was a sentence in white type *describing* a famous photograph.

"A three-year-old boy saluting at his father's funeral."

"A lone student standing in front of four tanks."

"An American President lifting his pet beagle up by the ears."

"A woman crying over the body of a student shot by the National Guard."

Instead of showing these famous photos, the negatives are developed in the reader's head. The reader *sees* JFK Jr. He *sees* Tienanmen Square. He *sees* LBJ and Kent State. "Hey, I know all these photos." The reader connects the dots and in doing so is rewarded for applying his intelligence, rewarded for staying with the ad. The client is rewarded, too, with a reader actively closing the loop between the famous photos and the cameras that took them.

Figure 3.11   Metaphors make intangible products, like banking, real.

In a great book called *A Smile in the Mind: Witty Thinking in Graphic Design,* authors McAlhone and Stuart say that "wit invites participation."

> [W]hen wit is involved, the designer never travels 100% of the way [toward the audience.] . . . The audience may need to travel only 5% or as much as 40% towards the designer in order to unlock the puzzle and get the idea . . . it asks the reader to take part in the communication of the idea. It is as if the designer throws a ball which then has to be caught. So the recipient is alert, with an active mind and a brain in gear.[9]

Their point about traveling "only 5% or as much as 40%" is an important one. If you leave too much out, you'll mystify your audience. If you put too much in, you'll bore them.

Testing the borders of this sublime area will be where you spend much of your time when you're coming up with ads. Somewhere between showing a picture of a flaming zebra on a unicycle and an ad that reads "Sale ends Saturday" is where you want to be.

The wisdom of knock-knock jokes.

Consider these one-liners from stand-up comedian Steven Wright: "If a cow laughed, would milk come out her nose? . . . When you open a new bag of cotton balls, are you supposed to throw the top one away? . . . When your pet bird sees you reading the newspaper, does he wonder why you're just sitting there staring at carpeting?"

Well, *I* think it's funny. In the last bit, for instance, the word "newspaper" begins as reading material and ends as cage-bottom covering. A shift has happened and now everything is slightly off. I don't know why these shifts and the sudden introduction of incongruous data make our computers spasm, they just do.

You may find that jumping from one point of view to another to introduce a sudden new interpretation is an effective way to add tension and release to the architecture of an ad. That very tension *involves* the viewer more than a simple expository statement of the same facts.

Creative theorist Arthur Koestler noted that a person, on hearing a joke, is "compelled to repeat to some extent the process of inventing the joke, to re-create it in his imagination." Authors McAlhone and Stuart add, "An idea that happens in the mind stays in the mind . . . it leaves a stronger trace. People can remember that flash moment, the click, and re-create the pleasure just by thinking about it."

A good example of this "click" is Chiat/Day's famous NYNEX television campaign.

One of the first NYNEX commercials opens on an easy chair set in a flat white background. Suddenly it's illuminated by the bright circle of a nightclub spotlight and "stripping music" begins to play. The chair begins to "undress." The doilies fly off, then the arm padding, finally the cushion covers. There's a fast cut to the NYNEX Yellow Pages as the camera whips in for a close-up of one of its many business categories: "Furniture Stripping." The book slams shut and a voice-over says: "The NYNEX Yellow Pages. If it's out there, it's in here."

"And that, dear students," said the professor of Humor 1001, "is why the chicken crossed the road." Suddenly, that's how this section feels to me. Pedantic. So I'll just close by saying that jokes make us laugh by introducing the unexpected. An ad can work the same way.

Don't set out to be funny. Set out to be interesting.

Funny is a subset of interesting. Funny isn't a language. Funny is an accent. And funny may not even be the right accent.

I find it interesting that the Clios had a category called "Best Use of Humor." And, curiously, no "Best Use of Seriousness." Funny, serious, heartfelt—none of it matters if you aren't interesting first. Howard Gossage, a famous ad person from the '50s, said, "People read what interests them; and sometimes it's an ad."

DON'T JUST DO AN AD.

Try not to sound like an ad.

Don't let your concept get in the way of the product. Bernbach said, "Our job is to sell our clients' merchandise . . . not ourselves. To kill the cleverness that makes us shine instead of the product." This can happen, and when a client kills an ad for this reason they may be right.

From more than one client, I've heard this dreaded phrase: "Your concept is a 'Visual Vampire.'" What they mean is the concept's execution seems so outrageous it sucks the life out of their commercial message. Be ready for it. Sometimes clients use the phrase as a bludgeon to kill something unusual they don't like. But on occasion, a few of them are right.

This usually happens when the product bores you. Which means you haven't dug deep enough to find the thing about it that's exciting or interesting. You settle for doing some sort of conceptual gymnastics up front and tacking your "boring old product" on the back side, hoping the interest from the opening will somehow bleed over to your sales message. But the interesting part of an ad shouldn't be a device that points to the sales message, it should *be* the sales message.

Go back. Rethink your strategy. Remember Bernbach's advice: "The product, the product, the product. Stay with the product." Don't get tangled up in unrelated ideas, however fanciful.

David Ogilvy used a classical reference to make this same point: "When Aeschines spoke, they said, 'How well he speaks.' But when Demosthenes spoke, they said, 'Let us march against Philip.'"

Try not to look like an ad.

People don't buy magazines to look at ads. So why look like one? This doesn't mean you should make it look like nonsense. Just try not to look like an *ad*. An ad says, "Turn the page."

Perhaps you don't need to stick a logo in the lower right-hand corner. Can you find another way to sign off? Can your TV spot look like documentary footage? Or a soap opera?

Your ad doesn't have to be a flat page.

Try a pop-up, a gatefold, a scratch and sniff.

Typically, liquor companies trot out these extravaganzas during the holiday season, spicing their inserts with talking microchips and pop-up devices. But there are less expensive tricks you can try.

Sequential ads or scratch-and-sniff concepts. Die-cuts. Different paper stock or acetate film. What can you do with the ad itself to make it more than just an ad?

One of the best I've ever seen was a little 2- by 4-inch flip-picture book, pasted to the middle of a white page, with the words "The Golf TDi Diesel" printed on the cover. When you flipped the pages you expected to see a little movie, a changing image of some kind. Instead, you saw a dashboard gas gauge with the needle staying, and staying, at "Full." The needle never moved. This little gem from BMP DDB Needham in London was a thing of beauty.

Your ad doesn't have to appear in a magazine.

Think creatively about different media where your message can appear. Just because the client's been running radio spots doesn't mean you need to write them.

The inside bottom of a paper coffee cup seems like a good place to put a message about sweeteners. A team at Kirshenbaum & Bond thought the sidewalks of New York City were a great place for a lingerie shop to stencil their message: "From here it looks like you could use some new underwear." And in London, Abbott Mead Vickers put this message from the business magazine, *The Economist,* on *top* of a bus (see Fig. 3.12).

Your idea doesn't even have to be an ad.

Two of the most fantastic selling concepts I've ever seen weren't ads per se.

One was for Mothers Against Drunk Driving. What they did was to park the wreckage of a car on the back of a flatbed truck and put it on display on a busy downtown sidewalk. It was a police car, one in which a Minnesota sheriff died at the hands of a drunken driver. Below the wreckage was a plaque with a description of the accident and the name of the law officer, a family man dead at the age of 36. No snappy headline. Just the ugly facts. And the car with its driver's side door punched in three feet. Nobody in that car could have lived. You could see it for yourself and you walked away mad.

*Figure 3.12   Your ad doesn't have to appear in the usual media.
Some of the best ones don't. This message from* The *Economist:
"Hello to all our readers in high office."*

The other example that comes to mind is British Airway's famous in-theater "performance."

Here's how they pulled it off. You're at the movie theater waiting for the show to start. You're eating your popcorn. On the screen appears what seems to be a boring destination commercial for an airline. It's a man and woman walking hand in hand down a street in Paris. You think, "Oh, *please.*" But suddenly, a woman out in the theater seats stands up and starts shouting at the screen.

"Bill? . . . *Bill?* What are you doing?" she yells. The man on the screen looks up, out at the audience, the fourth wall broken. He looks guilty. He should. He's been caught on camera with a girlfriend, cheating on his wife (or fiancée)—the woman in the audience. He tries to stutter some explanation. The theater-shrieker speaks her mind, grabs her coat, and storms up the aisle and out of the stunned theater.

Saatchi & Saatchi creatives closed this masterpiece with a voiceover suggesting, "Why not surprise *your* loved one with a British Airways [vacation] this weekend?"

That wasn't an ad. It was an event. And probably better than the movie.

SIMPLE = GOOD

If you take away one thing from this book, let it be the advice in this section. Simple is almost *always* better.

Maurice Saatchi, of London's M&C Saatchi, on simplicity: "Simplicity is all. Simple logic, simple arguments, simple visual images. If you can't reduce your argument to a few crisp words and phrases, there's something wrong with your argument. There's nothing long-winded about 'Liberté, égalité, fraternité.'"

"Simplicity, simplicity, simplicity!"

Henry David Thoreau, sitting in his shack by the famous pond, penned this oft-quoted line. Seems to me Hank needs a dose of his own medicine: "Simplicity, ~~simplicity, simplicity~~!"

Do the same with your ad. Look at this simple ad for Nike (Fig. 3.13). Every extraneous thing has been shaved away.

That reminds me. There's an old parable called Occam's razor. I don't know where it's from or how it went. I know only the moral. When you have two correct answers that both solve the problem,

Figure 3.13   Michelangelo said: "Beauty is the purgation of superfluities." I think Michelangelo would have dug this Nike ad, big time.

the more correct answer is the *simplest* one. Because it solves the problem with fewer moving parts. It solves the problem more elegantly.

"How difficult it is to be simple." —Vincent van Gogh

Simple is hard to miss.

I've always thought a stop sign is a perfect metaphor for a good ad. It makes me stop. It is relevant. It has one word. And most of all, it is simple. It says, "STOP."

It doesn't say, "Please bring your vehicle to a speed not exceeding zero miles per hour at this coordinate in space and time as there is other vehicular traffic moving in a direction perpendicular to your own and may intersect with your vehicle's current trajectory."

It says "STOP."

There is no introduction to stop. No asterisks are needed to understand stop. And stop needs no snappy wrap-up.

So how is a stop sign different from a good ad in a magazine? I'm turning the pages and suddenly right in my face is a big, simple, relevant message. How can I ignore it? This Japanese ad touting the safety of Volvo cars stopped me (Fig. 3.14).

Simple is bigger.

On May 7, 1915, a German U-boat sank a passenger ship, the *Lusitania,* killing some 1,190 civilians, many of them women and children. America was finally too angry to stay out of the Great War, and enlistment posters began to appear in shop windows, one of which is reprinted here (Fig. 3.15).

Most other World War I posters were not as visual and instead used headlines like "Irishmen, Avenge the Lusitania!" and "Take Up the Sword of Justice." Seems to me, all these decades later, they're not nearly as powerful as this one simple image, this one word.

Remember, in a cluttered TV or print environment, less is truly more. So have your radio spot be one guy saying 40 words. Have your print ad be all one color. Lock the camera down and do your

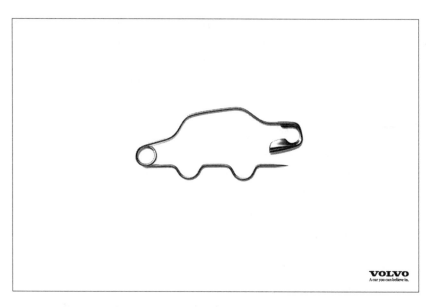

Figure 3.14   An ad produced in Japan by two guys named Masakazu Sawa and Minoru Kawase. The translation to English is perfect.

whole TV spot on a tabletop. Show a scorpion walking up a baby's arm. I don't know, but do something *simple.* Simple is big.

The artist Cézanne said, "With an apple, I will astonish Paris."

Simple is more believable.

A simple ad is more effective because there is less in it for a reader to object to. Fewer things to pick away at.

Presented with a simple ad, a reader sees less chance for duplicity or subterfuge. It's like a magician on a bare stage doing amazing tricks right before your eyes with no props and no curtains to hide behind.

Simple is easier to remember.

On a rainy November day in 1863, a U.S. senator named Edward Everett walked up to a podium and gave a two-and-one-half-hour speech consecrating a new cemetery. It was an impassioned speech, I'm sure, but I have been having trouble finding a transcript of this speech at the library.

Figure 3.15   After the Lusitania was torpedoed in 1915,
this incredible enlistment poster appeared. One word. One image.
No logo. And it still works.

The speaker that followed gave a 273-word speech, beginning with the words "Four score and seven years ago . . ."

Which of the two Gettysburg addresses given that day are you more familiar with?

Simple breaks through "advertising clutter."

If not with simplicity, how else would you make an ad break out of the cluttered TV or print environment? Should you do clutter that is more clever? Or perhaps clutter that has a better design? Clutter that is more strategically correct?

No. The only effective antidote to clutter is simplicity. How can anything else *but* simplicity break out of clutter?

Even the Super Bowl, with its annual collection of eye-popping TV commercials, has its own brand of clutter. Call it "good clutter" if you will, but it's still clutter, and you have to find a way to improve what a scientist might call its "signal-to-noise ratio." You have to break out. You can do that with an idea of sparkling simplicity.

McDonald's did it the year Burnett ran their famous baby-in-a-rocking-swing commercial on the Super Bowl. In that spot, viewers saw a baby crying in an odd rhythmic way that seemed to coincide with the downswing of his chair. You couldn't figure out why until the camera moved to reveal the baby's point of view. He was happy when the upswing let him see over the threshold of the windowsill—to a McDonald's sign across the street—and he cried when it was hidden from view. No words. Just a simple visual story.

Billboards force you to be simple.

In all of advertising, billboards are the best place to practice the art of simplicity. In fact, my first boss, Tom McElligott, told me if you have outdoor in the media mix for the campaign you're about to do, start there first. Nothing focuses you on a problem like this medium.

It's been said that a board should have no more than seven words. Any more and a passing motorist can't read it. But then you add the client's logo. One or two words. Now you're up to nine. And if your visual is something that takes one or two beats to understand, well, in my opinion, you've already got too much on your plate.

I suggest draconian measures. Shoot for three words, tops. It doesn't mean you'll be able to keep it to three. But start with three as your goal. The board pictured here (Fig. 3.16) works with just one word.

Keep paring away until you have the essence of your ad.

Let's start with three observations from three different men: one dead, one British, and one crazy.

Robert Louis Stevenson said, "The only art is to omit."

Tony Cox, a fabulous British writer: "Inside every fat ad there's a thinner and better one trying to get out."

And then there's Neil French, an absolutely stellar writer from Singapore. I met him one day, and he walked me through a wonderful exercise in the art of omitting, of reductionism.

He started by drawing a thumbnail sketch of a typical ad (#1 in Fig. 3.17). You have your headline, your visual, some body copy, a tag line, and a logo.

Okay, he asked, can we make this ad work without the body copy? Maybe we could do that by making the headline work a little harder. We can? Good, let's take out the body copy. That leaves the slightly cleaner layout of #2.

What about that tag line? Is it bringing any new information to the ad? No? Then let's broom it. Look, the third layout's even better.

Figure 3.16   This old 1960s billboard for Pan Am Airlines does its job with one word.

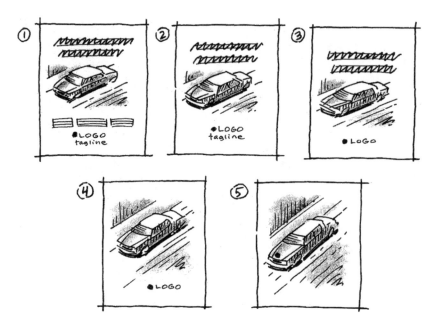

Figure 3.17   Neil's cool idea: reductionism. Ad #5 is almost always going to be better than ad #1.

Now, about that headline. Is it doing something the visual can't do? And that logo—isn't there some way we can incorporate it into the visual?

Ultimately, Neil reduced his ad to *one* thing. He suggested I do the same with my next ad. Get it down to one thing. Sometimes it's just a headline. Sometimes a picture. Either way, he said, the math always works out the same. Every element you add to a layout reduces the importance of all the other elements. And conversely, every item you subtract raises the visibility and importance of what's left.

I admit, this kind of reductionism is hard to pull off, especially when you have a client wanting to put more in an ad, not less. In my career I've done it only once. But to this day, that ad remains my favorite. It's the one you see here, reminding store buyers to stock Lee jeans (Fig. 3.18). No logo. No headline.

The less you have to put in the ad, the better. The writer Saki said, "When baiting a trap with cheese, always leave room for the mouse."

STICK A FORK IN IT. IT'S DONE.

Learn to recognize big ideas when you have them.

There will come a time when you see a great ad in a One Show annual, an ad that'll make you go, "Damn! I thought of that once!" It's a hard thing to see, "your" idea done and done well. That's why you have to be smart enough to pursue a promising idea once you've stumbled onto it. I'm reminded of a line by Ralph Waldo Emerson: "In every work of genius we recognize our own rejected thoughts."

See that one idea you have up on the wall? The one that's so much better than the others? Investigate why. There may be oil under that small patch of land. A big idea is almost always incredibly simple. So

Figure 3.18   It's hard to read reprinted here, but the little warning sign says: "This changing booth is monitored by store personnel to prevent theft, particularly theft of Lee jeans, the #1 brand of women, something that would really cheese off our store buyers, especially now that Lee has lowered their wholesale prices and the store stands to rake in some serious profit."

simple, you wonder why nobody's thought of it before. It has "legs" and can work in a lot of different executions, sometimes even in several media. Consider Goodby's "Got Milk?" campaign. Chiat's "Energizer Bunny." And Fallon McElligott's "Perception/Reality" for *Rolling Stone*. All simple. All huge.

Coming up with a big idea is one skill. Recognizing it is another. Develop both.

Big ideas transcend strategy.

When you finally come upon a big idea, you may look up from your pad to discover that you've wandered off strategy.

That's okay. The gold isn't always in them thar hills. But gold is gold, and good account executives will understand this and help you retool the strategy to get the client past this unexpected bump in the road.

My friend Mike Lescarbeau compares a big idea to a nuclear bomb. It doesn't have to land precisely on target to get the job done.

How you know when an ad is done.

Two observations, both stolen.

The first, from a book on creative theory called *Break Out!* by Dave Wallace.[10] He likens the final approach toward a perfect idea to the sounds made by different kinds of glassware. A so-so concept is like an ordinary jam jar. Hit it with your fingernail and you get an uninspiring "tung" sound. A good idea he likens to the sound of well-blown piece of glassware: a pleasing "tang." But a Waterford crystal idea, where you've done a thing perfectly, when all the molecules march in step and the stars align, there's that unmistakable "*ting*." Tung, tang, ting. Don't stop till you hear "ting."

Curiously, poet William Butler Yeats also used the metaphor of sound to convey perfection in an idea. He said the sound a good poem makes when it finishes is like a lid clicking shut on a perfectly made box.[11]

Don't keep running after you catch the bus.

After you've covered the walls with ideas and you've identified some concepts you really like, stop. And I mean *covered* the walls. This isn't permission to stop because you're tired or you have a few things that aren't half bad. It's a reminder to keep one eye on the deadline.

Blue-skying is great. You have to do it. But there comes a time (and you'll get better at deciding when) you'll have to cut bait and start working on the really good ideas. You have a fixed amount of time, so you'll need to devote some of it to making what's good great.

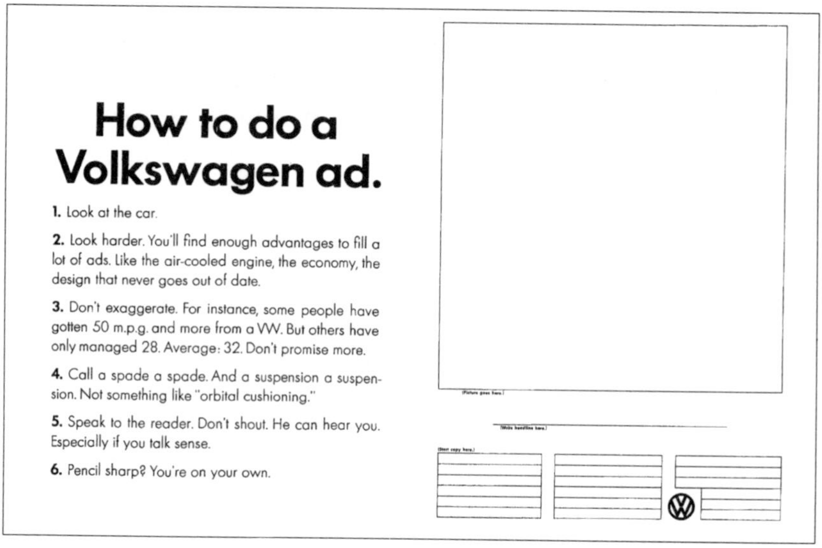

How to do a Volkswagen ad.

1. Look at the car.

2. Look harder. You'll find enough advantages to fill a lot of ads. Like the air-cooled engine, the economy, the design that never goes out of date.

3. Don't exaggerate. For instance, some people have gotten 50 m.p.g. and more from a VW. But others have only managed 28. Average: 32. Don't promise more.

4. Call a spade a spade. And a suspension a suspension. Not something like "orbital cushioning."

5. Speak to the reader. Don't shout. He can hear you. Especially if you talk sense.

6. Pencil sharp? You're on your own.

(Picture goes here.)

(Make headline here.)

(Start copy here.)

Ⓦ

Figure 4.1   A short course in copywriting from one of the best teachers in the world: Volkswagen.

4

Write When You Get Work

Making an ad—some finer touches

BEFORE WE BEGIN, A QUICK PIECE OF ADVICE: Learn to enjoy the process. Not just the finished ad. I used to hate the long process of writing an ad. I simply wanted the reprint in my hands. But thinking like this made my job harder than it had to be. The fact is, most of your time in this business will be spent in some cluttered, just-slightly-too-warm room, thinking, not admiring finished reprints pinned to your office wall.

Even if you have an award-winning career, only 0.00000002 percent of it will be spent walking up to the podium to accept an award at the One Show. You will spend most of your career trying to decide whether "crisp" or "flaky" is the right word to use. Keep reminding yourself of this. Let the fun be in the chase.

Come up with a lot of ideas. Cover the wall.

It's tempting to think that the best advertising people just peel off great campaigns ten minutes before they're due. But that is perception, not reality.

In fact, "Perception/Reality" (the famous *Rolling Stone* campaign from Fallon McElligott) is a perfect case in point. Those great ads that you may have seen in all the awards annuals are only the tip of the iceberg. The rest of it, a four-foot-high pile of other layouts, sat in writer Bill Miller's office for years. So massive was the pile of ideas, what he didn't use as ads actually served as a small table.

As a creative person, you will discover your brain has a built-in tendency to want to reach closure, even rush to it. Evolution has left us with circuitry that doesn't like ambiguity or unsolved problems. Its pattern-recognition wiring evolved to keep us out of the jaws of lions, tigers, and bears—not for making lateral jumps to discover unexpected solutions. But in order to get to a great idea, which is usually about the 500th one to come along, you'll need to resist the temptation to give in to the anxiety and sign off on the first passable idea that shows up.

Linus Pauling: "The best way to get a good idea is to get a lot of ideas. . . . At first, ideas seem as hard to find as crumbs on an oriental rug. Then they start coming in bunches. When they do, don't stop to analyze them; if you do you'll stop the flow, the rhythm, the magic. Write them down and go on to the next one."

Which leads to our next point.

Quick sketches of your ideas are all you need during the creative process.

Don't curb your creativity by stopping the car and getting out every time you have an idea you want to work out. Just put the concept on paper and continue moving forward. You'll cover more ground this way.

Tack the best ideas on the wall.

Seeing them up there all in a bunch helps you determine if there are campaigns forming and where holes are that need to be filled.

You keep working on the details on your pad. But up there on the wall the big picture begins to take shape.

Write. Don't talk. Write.

Don't talk to everybody about the concepts you're working on. Talking turns energy you could use to be creative into *talking* about being creative. It's also likely to send your poor listener looking for the nearest espresso machine because an idea talked about is never as exciting as the idea itself. If you don't believe me, call me up sometime and I'll describe the movie *Star Wars* to you.

There's an old saying: "A manuscript, like a fetus, is never improved by showing it to somebody before it is completed." Work. Just work. The time will come to unveil. For now, just work. The best ad people I know are the silent-but-deadly kind. You never hear them out in the hallways talking about their ideas. They're working.

Write hot. Edit cold.

Get it on paper quickly and furiously. Be hot. Let it pour out. Don't edit anything when you're coming up with the ads.

Then later, be *ruthless*. Cut everything that is not A-plus work. Put all the A-minus and B-plus stuff off in another pile you'll revisit later. Everything that's B-minus on down, put on the shelf for emergencies.

"The wastepaper basket is the writer's best friend." —Isaac Singer[1]

Once you get on a streak, ride it.

When the words finally start coming, stay on it. Don't break for lunch. Don't put it off till Monday. You'd be surprised how cold some trails get once you leave them for a few minutes.

Athletes call this place (where everything is working, where all the pistons are firing), they call it "the Zone." Some artists call it "the White Moment." I call it "that Brief Moment each week when I Don't Suck."

The moral: Never walk away from a hot keyboard (or drawing pad).

If it makes you laugh out loud, make it work. Somehow.

You know those really funny ideas you get that make you laugh and say, "Wouldn't it be great if we could really do that?" Those are often the very best ideas, and it is only your superego/parent/internalized client saying you can't do it. Revisit it. See if the objectionable element can be removed without hurting the concept.

Keep a file of images or ideas that strike your fancy.

I mean a real file, not a mental list of "I gotta do that someday." Keep a file, and every time you have an idea or see a scene in a movie that could be spun to your own purposes, scribble it down and throw it in.

My friend Dean Hanson was watching TV one night and saw some film of an elephant swimming, shot from underwater. He thought it was a beautiful image, taped the show, and put it on his shelf. Several years later he turned it into a great TV spot for Diet Coke. You can see the commercial in *Communication Arts,* December 1995.

HOW TO WRITE HEADLINES BETTER THAN THIS ONE.

Get puns out of your system right away.

Puns, in addition to be the lowest thing on the joke food chain, have no persuasive value. It's okay to think them. It's okay to write them down. Just make sure you toss them.

Don't just start writing headlines willy-nilly. Break it down. Do willy first. Then move on to nilly.

If you have an assignment that calls for a more verbal solution, don't just start spitting out the headlines. Instead, methodically explore different attributes and benefits of your product as you write.

Here's an example from my files. The project is a bourbon.

The client can afford only a small-space newspaper campaign and a billboard or two. They've said they want to see their bottle, so the finished ads will likely be just a bottle and a headline. After some discussion with the AEs about tone ("thoughtful, intellectual"), the art director and I consider several avenues for exploration.

The bourbon's age might be one way to go. Bourbon, by law, is aged a minimum of two years, often up to eight, sometimes longer. So we start there to see what happens. We put our feet up and immediately begin discussing the movie *The Terminator.* Sometime after lunch we take a crack at the "aging" thing.

AGE IDEAS

Order a drink that takes 9 years to get.

Like to hear how it's made? Do you have 9 years?

(*Note:* On the pages from the actual file, there are about five false starts for each one of these headlines. Tons of scratch-outs and half-witted ideas that go nowhere.)

9 years inside an oak barrel in an ugly warehouse. Our idea of quality time.

After 9 years of trickle-down economics, it's ready just in time.

Nine long years in a barrel. One glorious hour in a glass.

Okay, nine years. What else happens in nine years? What about the feeling of the slow passage of time?

Continental drift happens faster than this bourbon.

Mother Nature made it whiskey. Father Time made it bourbon.

We can't make it slow enough.

What wind does to mountains, time does to this bourbon.

On May 15th, we'll be rotating Barrel #1394-M one-quarter turn to the left. Just thought you'd like to know.

Tree rings multiply. Glaciers speed by. And still the bourbon waits.

Maybe one of these would work. There's another take on age we might try—namely, how long the *label's* been on the market. Not the age of the whiskey, but of the brand.

HISTORY-OF-BRAND IDEAS

First bottled when other bourbons were knee-high to a swizzle stick.

First bottled back when American History was an easy course.

First bottled when American History was called Current Events.

First bottled when the Wild West meant Kentucky.

Smoother than those young whippersnapper bourbons.

Back in 1796, this bourbon was the best available form of central heating.

The recipe for this bourbon has survived since 1796. Please don't bury it in a mint julep.

Write us for free information on what you can do with wine coolers.

We've been making it continuously since 1796. (Not counting that brief unpleasantness in the 1920s.)

If you can't remember the name, just ask for the bourbon first bottled when Chester A. Arthur was president.

110 years old and still in the bars every night.

If we could get any further behind the times, we would.

Are we behind the tymes?

A blast from the past.

Give Dad something older than his Sansabelt slacks.

First bottled before billboards.

This premium bourbon was first marketed via ox.

Introduced 50 years before ice cubes.

Okay, maybe there's some stuff we could use from that list. Maybe not. So far we've played with aging and brand history. What about where it's made?

KENTUCKY IDEAS

Kind of like great Canadian whiskey. Only it's bourbon. And from Kentucky.

Kind of like an old Kentucky mule. Classic, stubborn, and plenty of kick.

From the third floor of an old warehouse in Kentucky, heaven.

Warming trend expected out of Kentucky.

Now available to city folk.

If this ad had a jingle, it'd be "Dueling Banjos."

What the Clampetts would serve the Trumps.

This bourbon is the real McCoy. Even the Hatfields agreed.

It's not just named after a creek in Kentucky. It's made from it.

This is a beautiful picture of a tiny creek that flows through the
back hills of Kentucky. (Picture of bottle.)

Old as the hills it's from.

Smooth. Deep. Hard to find. Kind of like the creek we get the
water from.

Hand-bottled straight from a barrel in Kentucky. Strap in.

Tastes like a Kentucky sunset looks.

Its Old Kentucky Home was a barrel.

Maybe those last two would also make for good outdoor, given
how short they are. We make a note. Remember, the point here isn't,
hey, let's see how many headlines we can write, but rather how many
different doors we can go through. How many different ways can we
look at the same problem?

Okay, now let's see what can be done with the way some people
drink bourbon—straight. Or perhaps the time of day it's drunk.
(Wait a minute. Bad word.)

HOW-YOU-DRINK-IT IDEAS

With a bourbon this good, you don't need to show breasts in the
ice cubes. In fact, you don't need ice cubes.

Neither good bourbons nor bad arguments hold water.

Water ruins baseball games and bourbon.

Best. Enjoyed. Just. Like. This.

For a quiet night, try it without all the noisy ice.

Great after the kids are in bed. Perfect after they're in college.

Mixes superbly with a rocking chair and a dog.

You don't need water to enjoy this premium bourbon. A fire might
be nice.

Perfect for those quiet times. Like between marriages.

As you can see, each one of these doors we went through—age,
history, Kentucky—led to another hallway full of other doors to try.
Which is one of the marvelous things about writing. It's not simply a
way of getting things down on paper. Writing is a way of thinking;

thinking with your pencil, your wrist, and your spine and just seeing where a thing goes.

Clearly, a few of the bourbon ideas presented here aren't very good. (Lord knows, you may think they *all* stink.) But like Pickett's Charge at Gettysburg, with 15,000 soldiers, one or two are going to make it over the wall.

Don't let the headline flex any muscles when the visual is doing the heavy lifting.

As in dancing, one should lead, one should follow. If your visual is a hardworking idea, let your headline quietly clean up the work left to it. And if the headline is brilliant, well crafted, and covers all the bases, the visual (if one exists at all) should be merely icing on the cake.

Remember, the rule of thumb is never show what you're saying and never say what you're showing. This British ad for Volkswagen is a perfect example (Fig. 4.2). By itself, the visual is blind. By itself, the headline is dull. But together they make one of the best ads I've ever seen.

Certain headlines are currently checked out. You may use them when they are returned.

Lines like, "Contrary to popular belief . . ." or "Something is wrong when. . . ." These are dead. Elvis is dead. John Lennon is dead. Deal with it.

Remember, anything that you even *think* you've seen, forget about it. The stuff you've never seen? You'll know that when you see it, too. It raises the hair on the back of your neck.

Don't use a model number in the headline.

Client numbers like "TX-17" may seem familiar to you. But you're used to it; you work on the account. In a headline, they serve only as a speed bump. They're not words, they're numerals, and they force readers to switch gears in their heads to 17, 45, 82 to get through your sentence.

Figure 4.2   A perfect marriage of word and picture.

Never use fake names in a headline.

"Little Billy's friends at school call him different." Lines like this drive me nuts.

"Little Billy will never know his real father."

Hey, little Billy, come 'ere. Go back and tell your copywriter that a strange man in the park said to tell him he's a *hack*. Anybody reading this kind of crap knows these ad names are fake. And an irritating kind of fake at that. Like those manufactured relatives they put inside of picture frames at stores.

Provide detail.

In headlines, in body copy, anywhere you can say something specific and concrete, do it. It will make your argument more persuasive and your ad more interesting.

Here's an example of the power of detail. The headline read: "It began 400 years before Christ. It is visible from Mars. You can touch it this spring." Punctuated by a small picture of the Great Wall of China, the details in this headline made me keep reading about Royal Viking's cruises to China.

Avoid the formulaic version of saying one thing and showing another.

"Your kids deserve a licking this summer." . . . and then you have a picture of some kids with lollipops. Get it? Don't do this.

Again, this isn't a rule. But if you use this sort of setup, make sure the difference between word and picture is breathtaking. The polarity between the two should fairly crackle. This ad from Leagas-Delaney in London is a good example (Fig. 4.3).

WRITING OUTDOOR AND TRADE ADVERTISEMENTS

Outdoor is a great place to get outrageous.

Big as they are on the landscape, outdoor boards are an event, not just an ad. In fact, what makes for a good print advertisement doesn't necessarily make for a good billboard. Whatever you do,

*Figure 4.3   A very good example of picture playing off word,
done by two very naughty British boys.*

don't do something that's just "okay." A billboard's size only magni-
fies how "OKAY" your idea is. Be outrageous.

The boards pictured here (Fig. 4.4) qualify. Motorists had no idea
what the top board was all about when it went up, but there it was
just off the Long Island Expressway, bigger than life. A few weeks
later, when the finished board (bottom) went up, the payoff was
worth the wait.

A sidenote on billboards. When the Federal Highway Beautifica-
tion Act was passed in 1966, there were 42,601 billboards along the
highways here in Minnesota alone. Using the new federal law and
state rules, thousands of billboards were dismantled, leaving 4,827
by the time of this writing. Some days, I think that's still about 4,827
too many. Except for the handful I see in the One Show every year,
most billboards are mediocre or bad. When an ad in a magazine
sucks, I can turn the page. But if I live across the street from an ugly
billboard, there's nothing I can do about it.

Copywriter Howard Gossage didn't believe outdoor boards were
a true advertising medium: "An advertising medium is a medium that
incidentally carries advertising but whose primary function is to provide something else: entertainment, news, etc. . . . Your exposure to

*Figure 4.4 One execution from a wonderful campaign for NYNEX
Yellow Pages, done by Dion Hughes and Cabell Harris. The top board was
a teaser board that was posted, unexplained, for a week or two. On the
bottom, the board as it appeared several weeks later.*

television commercials is conditional on their being accompanied by
entertainment that is not otherwise available. No such parity or tit for
tat or fair exchange exists in outdoor advertising. . . . I'm afraid the
poor old billboard doesn't qualify as a medium at all; its medium, if
any, is the scenery around it and that is not its to give away."[2]

Until the day billboards are banned, either as "graphic littering" or
"retinal trespassing," you owe the citizens of the town where your
billboard appears your very best work. You must delight them.

Obscure trade ads are great assignments.

Trade ads typically run in tiny publications with titles like *Hose &
Nozzle World* and sell the services of one company to another.

When I first got into the business, I thought trade ads were somehow different than "regular" consumer ads. But they're not. They're a sales proposition, on paper, to a likely prospect. Trade ads are just as important to your client's economy as its consumer work, and they're usually a better gig than a consumer campaign. In fact, many clients don't seem to fuss as much over them. Trade ads seem to slip through the system a little faster. (In fact, consider that a rule of the business: The bigger the budget, the more client and agency layers you'll have to fight through.)

It's also likely that your trade assignment will have a cleaner playing field than a mass-market ad. There's a built-in villain: the other guy's product. The client will probably want you to take the gloves off. Which is fun.

There are many undiscovered opportunities in every agency's roster besides just the odd trade ad. Keep an eye out for them.

SOME NOTES ON DESIGN
(FROM A WRITER)

Something has to dominate the ad.

Whether it's a big headline, a large visual, or a single word floating in white space, somebody's got to be the boss.

It's easy to spot ads where the art director (or perhaps client) couldn't decide what was most important. The ads are usually in three big pieces. The visual takes up a third of the page. A headline takes up the next third. And a combination of body copy-logo-tag line brings up the rear. And the whole thing has about as much cohesion as a cookie in the rain.

Roy Grace, one of the famous art directors from Doyle Dane Bernbach, speaks to this issue:

> There has to be a point on every page where the art director and the writer want you to start. Whether that is the center of the page, the top right-hand corner, or the left-hand corner, there has to be an understanding, an agreement, and a logical reason where you want people to look first.[3]

Avoid trends in execution.

Don't take your cues from design trends you see in the awards books. (For one thing, if they're in the books, they're already two years old.) But this is about more than being up-to-date. It's about concentrating on the soul of an ad instead of the width of its lapels.

For instance, this trend of setting headlines with varying sizes of type. Or distressing type to the point of illegibility. To me, it's the typographical equivalent of the white disco suit John Travolta wore in *Saturday Night Fever.* It is a fad.

In addition to being a fad, over-art-directed typography distracts the reader by calling attention to the physical appearance of the words and, in doing so, slows down the reader's take on the ad, a process that should occur—bam!—just like that.

Before you try any gymnastics with ascenders and descenders, ask yourself: Is your typography directly contributing to the brand image? Is it an integral part of the message? Does it solve a problem? Does it make clearer what you're trying to say? If it does, good. If not, it's design trying to upstage the central idea and it doesn't belong in your ad. Get rid of it.

Chat cheerfully about one thing or another as you lead your overdesigned concept around to the back of the Type Barn. *("Yeah, Lennie, lookit them serifs. They sure is purdy.")* And shoot it in the head.

I know I sound like "Old Guy" when I talk like this. *("Well, when I was young, we set headlines in Futura Bold Condensed . . . and we LIKED it!")* You can do as you wish. I'll just warn you of two things. Riding the wave of every passing fad will make your portfolio look trendy and derivative. Also, when you enter the piece in a show and the judges see design getting in the way of an idea, which is precisely what this sort of posturing is, they'll deep-six it in a heartbeat.

Develop a look no one else has.

You've got to find something your client can call their own: a shape, a color, a design, something that is unique.

Helmut Krone: "I was working on Avis and looking for a page style. That's very important to me, a page style. I feel that you should be able to tell who's running that ad at a distance of twenty feet."[4]

What's interesting about Krone's statement is that he's not talking about billboards, but *print ads*. And if you look at his two most famous campaigns, they stand up to the test. You could identify his Volkswagen and Avis ads from across a street (Fig. 4.5).

When doing an ad that involves babies or children.

Always, *always* write the headline in the script of a child's handwriting. It's very cute, don't you think? And don't forget to have at least two of the letters adorably backward. E's are best. Backward O's don't work. O. See? (Just checking to see if you're awake.)

WRITING BODY COPY

Writing well, rule #1: Write well.

I don't think people read body copy. I think we've entered a frenzied era of coffee-guzzling, fax-sending channel surfers who honk the microsecond the light turns green and have the attention span of a flashcube. If the first five words of body copy aren't "May we send you $700?," word 6 isn't read. Just my opinion, mind you.

Raymond McKinney at The Martin Agency had it right when he wrote a line for those condensed-book study aids: "Cliff Notes. When you don't have time to see the movie."

Yet when I write body copy, long or short, I work hard at making it as smart and persuasive and readable as I can. I suggest you do the same. Because a few people are going to read it. And the ones who do, you *want*. They're interested. They're peering in your shop window.

So as much as I hammer away on the importance of visual solutions, when you have to write, write smartly. With passion, intelligence, and honesty. And when you've said what you need to say, stop.

Five rules for effective speechwriting from Winston Churchill.

1. Begin strongly.
2. Have one theme.
3. Use simple language.

Avis is only No.2 in rent a cars. So why go with us?

We try harder.
(When you're not the biggest, you have to.)
We just can't afford dirty ashtrays. Or half-empty gas tanks. Or worn wipers. Or unwashed cars. Or low tires. Or anything less than seat–adjusters that adjust. Heaters that heat. Defrosters that defrost.

Obviously, the thing we try hardest for is just to be nice. To start you out right with a new car, like a lively, super-torque Ford, and a pleasant smile. To know, say, where you get a good pastrami sandwich in Duluth.
Why?
Because we can't afford to take you for granted.
Go with us next time.
The line at our counter is shorter.

Figure 4.5   In an interview, art director Helmut Krone said that the Avis look came from a deliberate reversal of the VW look. VW had large pictures; Avis, small. VW had small body type, Avis, large. Note the absence of a logo.

4. Leave a picture in the listener's mind.

5. End dramatically.

Write like you talk.

In copy for ads, in letters to clients, and in memos to colleagues, write like you talk. For some reason, when handed a pen and asked to write something that will be seen by others, nine out of ten people decide an authoritarian tone is somehow more persuasive than clear English.

Consider this memo from my files. Were you to meet the man who wrote it, you'd say, "Sharp guy, that Bob. I want him on my account." Yet Bob wrote the following memo. (He was trying to say the program was killed because it was too costly.)

> Effective late last week the Flavor-iffic® project was shelved by the Flavor-Master Consumer Products Division Management.
>
> The reasoning had to do with funding generated covering cost of entry, not cost of entry as it would relate to test market in '95, but as it would relate to expansion, if judged successful across major pieces of geography in '96 and beyond.
>
> In sum, the way Flavor-Master new products division served up Flavor-iffic® to Consumer Products Division Management was that if Flavor-Master were to relax financial parameters for Flavor-iffic® in '95, '96, and '97, in effect have Corporate fund the program, Consumer Products Division could recommend to Corporate to proceed with the program. The decision was made at the Consumer Products Division Management level that Corporate would most probably not accept that and the subject was taken no further.

Except for the name "Flavor-iffic," I swear, every word of this memo is real.

The program was killed because it was too costly. That's nine words. Bob, in 143 words, was not only unable to get that nine-word message across, he effectively lobotomized his audience with a torrent of corporate nonsense that said nothing. It couldn't be decoded.

Bob proudly dictated this Rosetta stone, snapped his suspenders, and took the elevator down to the lobby thinking he'd done his bit to turn the wheels of capitalism for the day.

Yet when he got home, he probably didn't talk that way to his wife.

> Honey, RE: supper. It has come to my attention, and the concurrent attention of the other family members (i.e., Janice, Bill and Bob Jr.), that your gravy has inconsistencies of viscosity (popularly known as "lumps"), itself not a disturbing event, were it not for the recent disappearance of the family dog.

Write like you talk.

Write with a smooth, easy rhythm that sounds natural. Obey the rules of grammar and go easy on the adjectives. Short sentences are best. One-word sentences? Fine. End with a preposition if you want to. And if it feels right, begin a sentence with "and." Just be clear.

Through it all, remember, you are selling something. Easy to forget when you start slinging words.

Write like you would talk if you were the brand.

Every brand has a personality. You could describe Apple Computer's personality perhaps as "benevolent intelligence." Read the copy in any Apple ad from the last ten years and you'll feel like you're listening to the same smart older brother, one who wants to sit in the chair with you in front of the keyboard and show you how easy and smart and cool personal computers can be. Successful brands discover their own distinct voices and then stick with them year after year.

If you're inheriting an established voice, you can learn its cadences by reading their previous advertising. The planners on the account can also help school you in its accents.

If you have a new brand or you're creating a new voice for an old brand, consider yourself lucky. It's one of the most creative and rewarding things you can do in this business—discovering "who" a brand is and giving it shape and form and voice.

This isn't done to create stylish writing. What you're doing is creating a brand personality, an important point in a marketplace where the physical differences between products are getting smaller and smaller.

Let's say, for example, you're working on a car account. Most of the time, it's likely you'll have to show the car. Your ad may feel half art-directed already, and in a sense it is. So if it comes down to showing just a headline and a picture of a car, your headline ought to have a voice no one else does.

Here are three car headlines:

"If you run out of gas, it's easy to push."

"We'll never make it big."

"It's ugly, but it gets you there."

Here are three more:

"In a fuel-obsessed society, is it blasphemy to suggest that a car should be fun to drive?"

"A luxury sedan based on the belief that all of the rich are not idle."

"The people with money are still spending it, but with infinitely more wisdom."

Can you tell which ones are from Volkswagen and which from BMW? It's pretty easy. Which is as it should be.

Before you start writing copy, have the basic structure of your argument in mind.

Know where you're going to go. "Okay, I've got to come off that headline, then hit A, B, and then end on C." If you neglect this preparation, you will buzz about in a meaningless pattern, like a fly on a summer screen.

Don't have a what I call a "pre-ramble" in your body copy.

The first paragraph of copy in many ads is usually a waste of the reader's time, a repetition of what's already been said in the headline. Consider the analogy of a door-to-door salesman. Your headline is what he says through the crack in the door—his name, what he is selling, and why it's better than the other guy's stuff.

Okay, the reader's let you in. And now you're in the foyer. Don't waste time in your first paragraph being reintroductory. "Hi. Remember me? I'm the guy who was out in front of your door two seconds ago. Remember? Said my name, what I'm selling, and why it's better than that other guy's stuff?"

Get to the point. It's time for the details. Put your most interesting, surprising, or persuasive point in the first line if you can. You're lucky if people read your headline and luckier yet if they let you into the foyer by reading your copy.

Your body copy should reflect the overall concept of the ad.

When you start writing, borrow from your concept's imagery; lift colors from its palette. This advice isn't given for stylistic reasons. It helps keep the ad simple. One concept, one voice, one style.

Don't overdo this, a common mistake that leaves copy looking amateurish. Use it as you would a spice. In particular, resist the urge to do a "snappy" last line. I suggest ending with the client's address and phone number.

"It's not fair to inflict your own style on a strategy."

This is from Ed McCabe, one of the great writers of the 1970s. I think I know what he means.

Your job is to present the client's case as memorably as you can, not to come up with another great piece for your portfolio. What you want is to do both. But you aren't likely to do both if you're concentrating on style. Don't worry about style. It will be expressed no matter what you do. Style is part of the way your brain is wired. Concentrate on solving the client's problem well. The rest will just happen.

Eschew obfuscation.

My point exactly. Those words say what I mean to say, but they aren't as clear as they could be. This doesn't mean your writing has to be flat-footed, just understandable.

E. B. White said, "Be obscure clearly."

Pretend you're writing a letter.

Why write to the masses? It's one person reading your ad, isn't it? So write to one person.

Write a letter. It's a good voice to use when you're writing copy. It's intimate. It keeps you from lecturing. The best copy feels like a conversation, not a speech. One person talking to another. Not a corporate press release typed in the PR department by some guy named "Higgs."

Visualize this person you're writing the letter to. She's not a "Female, 18 to 34, household income of blah-blah." She's a woman named Jill who's been thinking about getting a newer, smaller car. She's in an airport, bored, trying to get a Gummi Bear out of her back tooth, and reading *Time* magazine backward.

Once you lay your sentences down, spackle between the joints.

Use transitions to flow seamlessly from one benefit to the next. Each sentence should come naturally out of the one that precedes it. When you've done it well, you shouldn't be able to take out any sentence without disrupting the flow and structure of the entire piece. (This fragile coherence of beautiful writing is lost on many clients and is one of the reasons copywriters are often seen mumbling to themselves at bus stops.)

Break your copy into as many short paragraphs as you can.

Short paragraphs are less daunting. I've never read William Faulkner's classic *Intruder in the Dust* for this very reason. Those eight-page paragraphs look like work to me. Remember, nobody ever had to read a *People* magazine with a bookmark. It's accessible. Make sure the copy in your ad looks the same way.

When you're done writing the copy, read it aloud.

I discovered this one the hard way. I had to present some copy to a group of five clients. I read it to them aloud. It was only during the act of reading it this way I discovered how wretched my copy was. Just hearing the words hanging out there in the air with their grade-school mistakes, seeing the flat reaction of the clients' faces, hearing my voice crack, the flopsweat, it's all coming back to me.

When you're done writing, read it aloud. Awkward constructions and wire-thin segues have a way of revealing themselves when read aloud.

When you're done ~~writing your body copy~~, go back and cut it by a third.

Don't dash off client-requested revisions and send the copy back.

When your copy comes back from the client with changes, don't just do patchwork at the point of impact. The whole piece may be out of alignment. Start from the top again, reread it all, and make sure any revision still has the flow of the original version.

Make your tag line an anthem.

If you *have* to craft a tag line, try to write about something bigger than just the client's product. Own some high ground.

In my opinion, the best ever written was for Nike: "Just Do It." That's not about shoes. It's not just about sports either; it's about life. Yet it sold a lot of shoes.

In addition to being cool because it's about more than just some product, an anthem allows you executional freedom later on when you may have to go in new tactical directions and still work off the same campaign.

Who says you have to have a tag line?

It's just one more thing to cram in an ad. One more element to clamor for attention. From what I see, few tag lines bring any new information to an ad. They're usually piffle.

"Looking Backward, but Poised Toward the Future, . . . Today."

"A Century of Excellence for Over 50 Years."

Should your client insist on a tag line, I refer you to this piffle-generation device John Lyons included in his book *Guts*.[5] "Simply pick one word from each column," he wrote, "string them together, and you've created a terrific corporate slogan."

systems	confidence	excellence
commitment	tomorrow	trust
spirit	achievement	technology
research	science	future
soaring	understanding	quality
mankind	helping	today
people	winning	innovations

"Commitment to an Understanding of Excellence." "The Spirit of Winning Through Quality." Ultimately, they're all the same.

In my opinion, unless you've penned a "Just Do It," just don't.

I once saw a tag line tragically misfire, injuring several. I think the line was for Stouffer's frozen entrées. The way Stouffer's wanted you to read it was: "People *Expect* Us to Be Better." But if you read, "People Expect Us to Be *Better*," it left a bad taste in your mouth.

Sweat the details.

Go to any length to get it right. Don't let even the *smallest* thing slide. If it bothers you even a little bit, work on it till it doesn't.

"A poem is never finished, only abandoned."   —Poet Paul Valery

Be objective.

Once you've put some good ideas on paper and had time to polish them to your satisfaction, maybe it's time to cart them around the hallways a little bit, even before you take them to your creative director. You're not looking for consensus here, just a disaster check.

This may not be your style and if you're not comfortable doing this, don't. But it can give you a quick reality check, identify holes that need filling, and point out directions that deserve further exploration.

Be objective. Listen to what people have to say about your work. If a couple of people have a problem with something, chances are it's real. Keep in mind when you're showing an ad around the agency, you're showing it to people who *want* to like it. Once your ad's out the door, it's quite the opposite. People will approach your ad thinking it's going to be as bad as everything else they see.

So listen to them. There's the old maxim: "When ten people tell you you have a tail, sooner or later, you have to turn around and look."

Kill off the weak sister.

If your campaign has even one weak ad in it, replace that "okay" ad with one that is as great as the others.

I have often talked myself into presenting campaigns that include weak sisters because time was running out. But readers don't care if most of your ads are great. They see them one at a time, so they all should be excellent.

There's a saying the Japanese use regarding the strict quality control in their best companies: "How many times a year is it acceptable for the birthing nurse to drop a baby on its head?" Is even one time okay?

There's another famous line. I don't know who wrote it. "Good is the enemy of great." It's true. Good is easy to like. Good throws its arm around you, says, "Hey, I'm not so bad, am I?" You talk yourself into it. Next thing you know you have a campaign that goes, great—great—good. And that's bad.

———

WHAT TO DO IF YOU'RE STUCK.

Leave the room and go work somewhere else.

A conference room maybe. Or leave the agency. Work in a public place. Some restaurants are close to empty between one and five. Hotel lobbies are great, especially those lobbies on the second floor that looked really sharp and modern on the architect's drawing but nobody *ever* uses.

If the print isn't coming, work on the radio. If you can't write the headline, write body copy. If your pen isn't moving, try typing.

And if it's not happening during office hours, stop in the middle of supper and write.

"If you are in difficulties with a book, try the element of surprise: attack it at an hour when it isn't expecting it." —H. G. Wells.

Go to the store where they sell the stuff.

There is demographic data typed neatly on paper. And there is the stark reality of a customer standing in front of a store shelf looking at your brand and at Brand X. I'm not saying you should start bothering strangers in store aisles with questions. Go ahead if you like. I find it inspiring just to soak in the vibes of the marketplace. Just watch. Think. I guarantee you'll come back with some ideas.

Ask your creative director for help.

That's what they're there for. There is no dishonor in throwing up your hands and saying, "I'm in a dark and terrible place. Help me or I shall perish."

Your CD may be able to see things you can't. He hasn't had his nose two inches away from the problem for the last two weeks like you have. He knows the client, knows the market, and can give you more than an educated guess on what's jamming up your creative process. Sometimes all it takes is a little push, two inches to the left, to get you back on track.

Get more product information.

You may not know enough about the problem yet, or you may not have enough information on the market. So ask your AEs or planners to go deeper into their files and bring you new stuff. It's likely they edited their pile of information and gleaned what they thought most important. Get to the original material if you can.

If you're stuck, relax.

Most of the books I've read on creativity keep bringing the subject up. You can't be creative *and* be tense. The two events are never in the same room together. Stay loose. Breathe from the stomach. If you're not relaxed, stop until you are. Just the simple act of physical relaxation will bring on new ideas. I promise.

But remember, you do need a certain amount of pressure to be creative. Creativity rarely happens when things are perfectly under control. To make the kettle boil, a little fire is necessary, and a deadline that's a month and a half away isn't always a good thing. I find that if I have too much time to complete a project, I'll put off working on it until two or three weeks before it's due just so I can dial up the pressure a little bit.

The trick is to control the pressure, not let it control you. Relax.

If you're stuck, relax—part 2.

You may not actually be stuck. You just think you're stuck because you're editing yourself too harshly. You have ideas but you're not sharing them with your partner or even writing them down. Maybe you've set your bar too high. Lower it. Don't be afraid to make big, fat mistakes. Lighten up. Have fun. It's just advertising.

Read an old *Far Side* collection by Gary Larson.

The man is an absolute screaming genius. The cartoons are always funny. But look at the economy of his ideas. Look how simple they are. How few moving parts there are.

At the very least, with a trip to Larson's sick, twisted world you get a break from the tension. But you might get that little nudge you need. I know I have.

I also get that nudge by leafing through magazines from different categories. I'll be working on an insurance campaign, but if there's a snowboarding magazine on the conference-room table, I'll pick it up and go through it.

Leafing through the awards annuals is okay, too. Get some inspiration, but don't stay there too long. The shows are a good learning tool early in the business; they're a good starting point early in the ideation process. But at some point, they will begin to steer your thinking. Sooner or later, you're going to have to unmoor and sail into the unknown.

Sometimes it's good to work on three projects at once.

You may find that the ideas come faster if you move between projects every hour or so. Designer Milton Glaser said, "Working on one thing at a time is like facing a rhinoceros; working on ten things at a time is like playing badminton."

Don't burn up too much energy trying to make something work.

Follow the first rule of holes: "If you are in one, stop digging." There's a book called *Lateral Thinking* by Edward DeBono. His metaphor—don't dig one hole and keep digging down until you hit oil. Dig lots of shallow holes first, all over the yard.

Even when you do manage to force a decent idea onto paper after hours of wrestling with it, it usually bears the earmarks of a fight. There are embarrassing dents where you pounded on the poor thing to force it into the shape you wanted. There's none of the spontaneous elegance of an idea born in a moment of illumination.

Be patient.

Tell yourself it will come. Don't keep swinging at the ball when your arms hurt. Maybe today's not the day. Give up. Go see a movie. Come back tomorrow. Pick up the bat and keep trying. Be patient.

Visualize yourself getting the idea.

You know all those books in the "self-help" section at the bookstore? With those corny titles like "*You Can Sell Anything!!*" There must be 800 titles and I can save you about $1,000 by telling you what everybody underlines somewhere in every one of these books: <u>Visualize yourself successfully doing it.</u> It's that simple. And it works.

Please send me the $1,000 you didn't spend, care of the publisher. Thank you.

Remember that you aren't saving lives.

When you get stressed and the walls are closing in and you're going nuts trying to crack a problem and you find yourself getting depressed, try to remember that you're just doing an ad. That is all. An *ad*. A stupid piece of paper. It's not even a whole piece of paper you're working on. It's just a half of a piece of paper in a magazine and somebody else is buying the other side. Remember, advertising is powerful, and even a "pretty okay" ad can increase sales. (I know, I know. Don't tell my clients I said this. But we're talking those times when it feels like your mental health is at stake.) Don't kill the goose trying to get a golden egg on demand.

Bertrand Russell said: "One of the symptoms of an approaching nervous breakdown is the belief that one's work is terribly important."

INSANITY, OFFICE POLITICS, AND AWARDS SHOWS

"Be orderly in your normal life so you can be violent and original in your work."

I don't know who said this great line, but it seems to fit in right about here.

Many creative people find that a dash of ritual in their lives provides just the structure they need to let go creatively. I happen to prefer an extremely clean and empty room in which to write. That may sound weird, but I've heard of stranger things.

In *The Art and Science of Creativity,* George Kneller wrote: "Schiller [the German poet] filled his desk with rotten apples; Proust worked in a cork-lined room. . . . While [Kant was] writing *The Critique of Pure Reason,* he would concentrate on a tower visible from his window. When some trees grew up to hide the tower, [he had] authorities cut down the trees so that he could continue his work."[6]

Your office manager may not like it, but if some trees are bugging you, hack those suckers down.

Be buttoned-up.

This is a business. The whole chaos-is-good, whiskey-and-cigarettes, showing-up-late-for-work thing is fine for artists and rock stars. But advertising is only half art. It's also half business. The thing is, both halves are on the deadline.

So don't be sloppy. Don't be late. Meet your deadlines. Don't lose your writer's headlines. Don't leave your art director's lay-outs at home. Don't forget to do the outdoor because the print is more fun.

This also applies to expense reports and time sheets. Learn how to do them early on, do them impeccably, and turn them in on time. Be a grown-up. Sure they're boring. But, like watching an episode of *The Brady Bunch,* if you just sit down and apply yourself, the whole unpleasant thing will be over in a half hour.

One last piece of advice: Take great care of original pictures or negatives lent to you by clients or photographers. I once saw an agency pay a $50,000 fee because an art director couldn't find one little 35mm negative.

Don't drink or do drugs.

You may think that drinking, smoking pot, or doing coke makes you more creative. I used to think so.

I was only fooling myself. I bought into that myth of the "tortured creative person," struggling against uncaring clients and blind product managers. With a bottle next to his typewriter and his wastebasket filling ever higher with rejected brilliance, this poor, misunderstood soul constantly looks for that next fantastic idea to rocket him into happiness.

In a business where we all try to avoid clichés, a lot of people buy into this cliché-as-lifestyle. I can assure you it is illusion.

Identify your most productive working hours and use them for nothing but idea-generation.

I happen to be a morning person. By 3:00 in the afternoon, my brain is meat loaf and a TV campaign featuring a grocer named Whipple doesn't seem like such a bad idea to me. But you might be sharper in the afternoon. Just strike while your iron is hot. And save those down hours for the busywork of advertising. What I call "phone calls and arguments."

Keep your eye on the ball, not on the players.

Don't get into office politics. Not all offices have them. If yours does, remember your priorities—doing ads. Keep your eye on the ad on your desk.

You are a member of a team.

Don't ever forget that. Never get into that "I did the visual" or "I did the headline" thing. You work as a team, you lose as a team, you win as a team.

You are not genetically superior to account executives.

During my first years in the business I was trained to look down on AEs. At the time, it seemed kind of cool to have a bad guy to make fun of. *("Oh, he couldn't sell a joint at Woodstock." "She couldn't sell a compass to Amelia Earhart.")* But I was an idiot. It's wrong to think that way. They are on my side. Make sure they're on yours.

Stay in touch with the real world.

Jerry Della Femina, an old boss of mine, put it this way:

> Young creative people start out hungry. They're off the street; they know how people think. And their work is great. Then they get successful. They make more and more money, spend their time in restaurants they never dreamed of, fly back and forth between New York and Los Angeles. Pretty soon, the real world isn't people. It's just a bunch of lights off the right side of the plane. You have to stay in touch if you're going to write advertising that works.[7]

So, stay in touch. One way to do that is to watch TV all the time. (Is this a great business or what?)

"What are you doing, honey?"

"Oh, I'm in here analyzing the psyche of my culture—absorbing the Zeitgeist, as it were. I can't be bothered."

Read books and magazines. See all the movies. Go to the weird new exhibits at the museums. Know what's out there, good and bad.

It's called keeping your finger on the pulse of the culture, all of which has direct bearing on your craft. (Also, don't forget, come the ides of April, you may be able to deduct from your income all subscriptions, video rentals, cable bills, and movies.)

On the value of awards shows.

I shouldn't talk. In my younger days, I was a pathetic awards hound. Just around April, you'd find me lurking in the mail room pining for "the letter" from the One Show announcing accepted entries. "Is it here yet? . . . Well, check *againnnnnn*."

But I won't be too hard on myself. Our work isn't signed. And when you're new in the business, there's no better way to make a name for yourself than getting into "the books." Awards shows allow tiny agencies to compete with the behemoths. They serve as great recruiting tools for agencies. And they expose us to all kinds of work we'd not see otherwise. So I recommend them. With some caveats.

Don't make the wrong name for yourself by entering too many campaigns for easy, microscopic, or public-service clients. They might get in.

Don't talk about awards shows around clients or account executives. You'll devalue yourself in their eyes and make your work suspect. *("Is that last ad she did on strategy or is it just another entry into Clever-Fest?")*

Don't enter every show. As of this writing, there are 39 different national awards shows in this industry. No kidding—*thirty-nine*. And that's not counting the local shows. Only a few of these shows have merit. In my opinion, the best are the One Show and *Communication Arts*. And, in England, D&AD.

Open on the coast of Scotland. Pan to Sigourney Weaver mohawked and saddled on a breaching whale. Using only a blowgun and a flare, she takes out every Russian whaling ship in the Atlantic. It's action. It's 90's. It's Eco-Aliens with a Gorillas In The Mist twist. Of course, there'll be shark-related casualties and heavy gunfire.

| All locations for this blockbuster can be found in Oregon. Call David Woolson at the Film & Video Office, 5o3-373-1232. |

Oregon. Things look different here.

Figure 5.1   If print advertising is the book, television is the movie.

5

In the Future, Everyone Will Be Famous for 30 Seconds

Some advice on making television commercials

PEOPLE GENERALLY GET INTO THIS BUSINESS learning their craft on print ads. But you'll find as you grow, you need to start doing more and more TV. To advance, you'll have to do it well.

It's been said, "Great print can make you famous. Great TV makes you rich." There's some truth in it. National television campaigns are where the big agencies make most of their money. The people who can turn out great TV often command the highest prices.

Many of the suggestions from the chapters on writing print ads apply to this medium, the virtues of simplicity being perhaps the most important. Here are a few other things I've learned from my colleagues along the way.

CREATING THE COMMERCIAL

Rule #1 in producing a great TV commercial. First, you must write one.

It takes exactly as much work to produce a bad TV spot as a good one. If you have a so-so storyboard approved, you're going to put in the same hours producing it that they put in making Apple's famous "1984" commercial (Fig. 5.2).

The writer's job on a TV spot doesn't end with coming up with the idea. That's just the beginning of a long process, a process you'll play a part in all along the way. Sell a so-so print idea and at least you'll have the thing out of your hair relatively quickly. A so-so TV spot will haunt you for weeks. You'll have the same long casting sessions as you would producing a great spot, the same boring hours on the set during prelighting, and the same cold coffee in the editing suites. But when you're done, you'll have a ho-hum commercial.

Put in the hours now, during the creative process. Make the concept great. Otherwise you will have a long time to wish you did.

Make sure you know what kind of money is available for your project before you start.

It's no fun to waste time coming up with a great campaign the client can't afford. So ask your account people to provide a real production estimate. Don't let them tell you the client doesn't really know. That's like walking into a Mercedes dealership and telling the salesperson you "don't really know" how much you have to spend. *("I might have $60,000 . . . I might not. I don't really know.")*

Typically, production estimates are 10 percent of the total media buy. Getting this figure is sometimes difficult, but *somebody somewhere* at the client has a dollar amount in his head and it's best you find out what it is now.

Remember, just because you can think it up doesn't mean you can shoot it.

Before you get too excited about selling an idea, make sure your idea can be executed within your budget. Even the simplest effects can be surprisingly expensive, and some are hard to pull off regard-

Figure 5.2 $^1/_{1,440}$ of Chiat/Day's famous "1984" commercial for Apple Computers. A recent customer survey named it the best commercial of all time. For a few more frames, as well as all the copy, see the One Show, volume 6.

less of the money available—particularly if they involve animals, children, or water.

Study the reels.

There's nothing like seeing a great commercial on a real television screen. Commercials don't make the transition to the printed page very well. (That's why I've included only a few stills from favorite commercials in this chapter.) You need to see the reels.

There are a lot of them out there. There's the annual Cannes reel. There are the reels from the One Show and *Communication Arts.* You can also get reels from directors and effects houses, as well as private labels like "Shots" and "Archive." Ask your producers to help you keep up on what's new.

Stay abreast, too, of who's shooting the hottest music videos. There's a lot of churn in this industry, with new people coming in all the time: independent filmmakers, students out of school, still photographers moving into film. A sharp producer can help keep you up-to-date.

Solve the problem visually.

TV is a visual medium and it begs for visual solutions. Try to avoid verbal approaches. Don't talk at customers. Tell them a story with pictures. Start with images. Stay with images.

There is a saying: "The eye will remember what the ear will forget." Remember the last time you tried to tell somebody about a great commercial you'd seen? Did you recite the script? Or paint a picture?

Can you make the picture do all the work?

Let your TV concept be so visually powerful that a viewer would get it with the sound turned off. This isn't a rule; it doesn't always work. But when it does, it's great. It means you have a very simple, very visual idea.

This Maxell audiotapes commercial from the 1970s said it all with one image (Fig. 5.3). A guy listening to music on a Maxell tape is literally blown away by the fidelity and power of the sound. You could have been vacuuming your living room when this spot came on and you'd still get it.

Find one great image and build a story around it.

Try looking at your TV assignment as a print job. If you had to settle on a single image to convey your point, what would it be? Once you've found that image, trying spinning a story into or out of it.

Start with a shooting technique and back it into a concept.

Start with an execution—a film style, a special effect, an incredible look of any kind—and then work backwards to a concept. This is tricky territory because you need to come out on the other side with an idea. But we're talking about TV, where image is king. So if you have some new vision in your head, or you've seen a fabulous technique in a movie or in a music video, try to bend it to your client's purposes. It's sort of a "Fire!, Aim, Ready" thing, but if you end up with a cool concept, who cares which door you came in?

Figure 5.3   One image tells the sales story without words. Maxell's still using this image 20 years later, selling video- as well as audiotape.

Be simple.

The advice about staying simple applies to TV as it does to print. And nowhere does it apply more than in low-budget commercials.

If you've been assigned a cheapo TV spot, congratulations. It's going to force you to pare away the dross and get to the essence of the client's marketing problem. So valuable is this kind of thinking, you should start here even if your client has a large budget.

The Martin Agency's John Mahoney and Hal Tench did a great (and very simple) commercial for an agricultural pesticide using two hammers set on a white tabletop (Fig. 5.4). One hammer appeared to be forged out of gold; the other, iron. Next to the hammers, two bugs. A voice-over said, "You have your expensive insecticide." (Hand comes in, picks up gold hammer, smashes bug.)

"And your cheap insecticide." (Hand comes in, picks up iron hammer, smashes bug.)

"So," concluded the voice-over, "which worm is more dead? Ammo. Guaranteed worm control. Cheap."

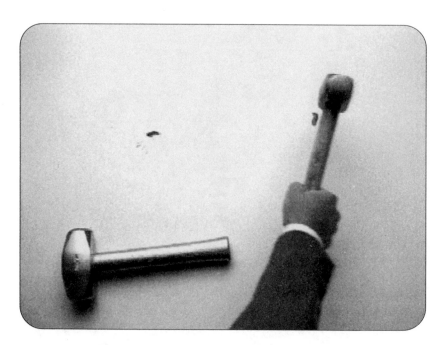

Figure 5.4 If the creative team had five times the budget, they couldn't have improved on this simple, wonderful commercial.

If you can make the first two seconds of your spot visually unusual, do so.

Think about it. Your viewer's watching TV. His eyes are glued to it. The cop shoots the bad guy in the head. The camera closes in. Oh, no! He shot his partner. Fade to black. You now have two seconds to keep the viewer's eyes on the screen before he heads to the kitchen to eat chili out of the can over the sink.

This famous spot for Honda automobiles would probably keep him in his seat (Fig. 5.5). The first image is remarkable—a car is hanging on a museum wall like a painting. It stays there until a museum visitor admires it enough to open the door, walk up the wall, get in and drive away. It was hard *not* to watch.

A television commercial must entertain throughout the entire spot.

Avoid long buildups to an "unexpected" conclusion, or a what I call a "waw-waw" (*Leave It to Beaver* music) ending. This is often called

Figure 5.5   Open strong. You're competing against getting a second bag of Orange Cheeze Kurls, or going to the bathroom. Formidable competition.

"doing a print idea on TV." A lot of people do it and it's a mistake to the degree that it doesn't take full advantage of the medium.

Once you know a commercial's "unexpected" ending, how many more times will you really enjoy watching it? A great spot, say from Nike or Little Caesar's, is a joy to watch from beginning to end, over and over. There's something new to look for in each frame.

If you can demonstrate your product on TV, do it.

Nothing beats actually seeing it with your own eyes. You can't always do a demonstration, and, clearly, there are great commercials out there that aren't demos. But when they work, they *really* work. The trick is to demonstrate the product in an unexpected, memorable way.

One great example comes to mind: the Penn tennis balls commercial from Fallon McElligott (Fig. 5.6).

The strategy: consistent performance from ball to ball.

The slogan: "You've seen one, you've seen them all."

The demonstration: The chairman of Penn drops three of his company's tennis balls from a tall building, while the chairman of the competition looks on, waiting his turn. Each Penn ball can be seen bouncing exactly the same height after impact. The voice-over concludes, "Then we try the same test with our competitor." That's when the other chairman is pitched over the railing.

Don't force your TV to look like your print.

A lot of the bigger clients insist on this, saying that identical print and TV executions will give them a "synergy." If your print also happens to work as great TV, fine. But if it doesn't, don't let them force you to drag an idea kicking and screaming from one medium into another.

All you should promise the client is the campaign will have one voice, one message, across all media—not an unfair request, not an unfulfillable promise. But if your TV sounds like David Letterman and your print reads like the *Wall Street Journal,* your campaign isn't holding together.

Figure 5.6   A great product demonstration from Penn tennis balls.
"Then we try the same test with our competitor."

Think in campaigns.

Even if your assignment is a one-shot, think long term. There is power in a campaign idea that even the best one-shots will never have.

Your campaign thread can be almost anything: a comic bit (Little Caesar's stretchy cheese), austere art direction (Honda), a visual device (the Energizer Bunny), or a person (Nissan's "Mr. K." and Snapple's receptionist, Fig. 5.7). Think visually. But also think big.

A FEW THOUGHTS ON WRITING FOR TV

Write sparely.

Don't carpet your spot with wall-to-wall copy. Leave breathing room. Lots of it. After you've written your script, get out a really big, scary knife. Like the one in *Halloween 4*.

Figure 5.7   Think in campaigns. For Snapple, the creative team had one idea: the Snapple receptionist answers letters. And the campaign ran (and ran) from there.

You'll be glad you did, come editing time. You'll find you need space to let those wonderful moments on film just happen by themselves, quietly, without a voice-over jabbering in your ear.

Author Sydney Smith suggested, "In composing, as a general rule, run your pen through every other word you have written; you have no idea what vigor it will give to your style."

For 15-second spots, write very, very sparely.

Ten- or fifteen-second TV spots are a different animal than a thirty. You have no time for a slow build. With four to five seconds already set aside for the wrap-up and client logo, you're looking at ten very skinny seconds to unpack your show, put it on, and hit the showers.

So strip your 15-second TV spots down to the bones. And then strip again down to the marrow. Lock off the camera and keep it to one scene if you can. Even two cuts can make a 15 look choppy.

Figure 5.8 is a just one frame of a 15-second Federal Express spot. But you're not missing much seeing it this way. The camera was locked down and never moved off of the whimpering little man cow-

Figure 5.8   Fifteen-second spots are like video billboards.
They have to happen fast.

ering in his boss's shadow. No cuts. Just the little man saying: "I'm sorry, Mr. Dinger, they told me they'd get the package there by tomorrow, Mr. Dinger, and I believed them and they made me look bad, Mr. Dinger."

Never show what you're saying and never say what you're showing.

This idea, discussed in print advertising, has a counterpart here in broadcast, with a few twists.

You have two tracks of information in a TV spot occurring simultaneously: audio and visual. To some degree, they have to match up. If either track wanders too far afield of the other, the viewer will not know which to attend to, lose interest, and begin feeling around in the couch for change. On the other hand, you don't want to have the voice-over and video so joined at the hip that the viewer hears again what he's already seeing on screen.

It's better to have one track complete the other, or play off the other, just as you do in print. That $1 + 1 = 3$ thing works to great effect here in television. The words and the visuals can supply slightly different pieces of information, tracks that the viewer can integrate in his head.

Sometimes you can add creative tension between what is seen and what is heard by giving the copy an unexpected tone, perhaps of irony or understatement. For instance, I remember a Reebok spot featuring a popular Dallas Cowboy running-back crashing into defensive players. What you heard, though, was the player quietly musing about how football "allows you to meet so many people."

STORYBOARDING YOUR SPOT

Make sure your storyboard runs by itself, without training wheels and without you running along beside it explaining everything.

A storyboard is a visual map of the commercial. A series of illustrations that show the action of the spot with copy below each frame describing the action and what the voice-over says. (For an example, see Fig. 5.9.)

1.) OPEN ON A GIANT NIKE PAINTED BUILDING SIDE OF FRENCH SOCCER STAR, SOMEWHERE IN PARIS.

2.) A GIANT BALL COMES OUT OF NOWHERE, ROCKETING TOWARDS SOCCER STAR.

3.) THE PAINT COMES TO LIFE AND SOCCER STAR DEFTLY RECEIVES THE BALL, SETS IT UP, AND . . .

4.) . . . KICKS IT, OFF AND OUT OF THE BUILDING, FORCING SOME BRICKS TO EXPLODE.

5.) WE FOLLOW THE BALL OFF THE BUILDING, OVER A SEA, AND BALL ARRIVES IN GERMANY.

6.) WHERE FAMOUS GERMAN SOCCER PLAYER STOPS THE BALL WITH HIS CHEST, AND THEN . . .

Figure 5.9   This storyboard (shortened by half to fit this format) is for one of Wieden & Kennedy's best spots for Nike. Called "The Wall," and shot by Joe Pytka, this commercial won just about every award in 1994, including Best of Show in the One Show.

Storyboards used to be the only way TV was presented to clients, but agencies are moving away from them now. Many clients can get tripped up by minor details that have more to do with how the commercial is drawn than how it will be shot. Presentations are now more often a matter of talking a client through an idea. Sometimes a

7.) . . . SENDS IT OFF IN A HAIL OF BRICKS TO. . .

8.) . . . ROME, WHERE POPULAR ITALIAN PLAYER OUTJUMPS OPPONENTS TO SEND A ROCKET HEADER . . .

9.) . . . OVERSEAS TO LONDON, WHERE . . .

10.) . . . FAMOUS ENGLISH PLAYER FLIPS OVER FOR A PERFECT BICYCLE KICK . BALL GOES THROUGH THE BRICKS . . .

11.) . . . OVERSEAS TO MEXICO CITY, WHERE FAMOUS GOAL KEEPER TRIES TO BLOCK KICK.

12.) KEEPER LEAPS ACROSS SEVERAL BUILDING FACES, BUT CAN'T BLOCK PERFECT KICK TO CORNER.

single "key frame" is put on the wall during a presentation, but the overall concept is presented with words, gestures, and performance.

But sooner or later you're going to need to send your idea out into the world—to distant clients, to directors, to network approval committees—and you'll need to do a full board. And since it's likely you'll have to send it off to these places, unaccompanied, your board should speak for itself.

So make it simple. Make it clear. Make sure the story unfolds, A, then B, then C.

Compose every frame of the board to telegraph to the viewer what is important about that scene. Each frame should include enough information to advance your story, and no more. The board should feed a viewer information, piece by piece, with each shot building on the one that precedes it.

Make sure your final board communicates and entertains.

As you make your final board, revisit the whole concept. And this time give attention to the details.

Is the opening frame interesting enough? Should the camera be at a different angle? Is the location just right? Are you giving away too much in the beginning of the spot? Can you cut into a scene later? Can you simplify anything? Does your spot have too many cuts? Can you economize and make one scene solve two problems? Is the story told coherently?

Now's the time to make these enhancements, before you show it to the client. I've found that after a client signs off on something, they don't much like changes, even improvements.

This is an important point. Once a client has sold your idea up the line to the boss and the boss's boss, it's etched in stone. You'll have more luck trying to get into the vaults at the National Archive to scribble some changes on the U.S. Constitution. *("No, officer, you don't understand. I just need to make a few teensy changes. See, they spelled 'Congress' with 'f's.' So it reads 'Congreff.' We think it looks kind of . . . ftupid. So let me in, please. I'll just . . . let GO of me!")*

Make sure the mechanics of your storyboard actually work.

I know some creative teams who do 30-frame storyboards. They lay out the architecture of the entire spot, second by second.

Another effective way to see if your spot flows is to do what's called an "animatic"—a sort of filmed-storyboard, animated version of your spot. Unfortunately, many clients force agencies to make these silly cartoons so they can drag the poor things into testing. (Always a bad idea, but more on that in Chapter 9.)

But at the very least, an animatic gives you a chance to mess around with your commercial's structure and timing before you go into production. You can get answers to questions like, when does the voice-over come in? When does the music come up and go down? Is there time during each scene to read the copy that goes with it?

Since any animatic you do is never going to look much better than a bad cartoon, you might consider spending some money on a high-class voice-over as well as some great music. (It's sort of like settling for a date who doesn't look very good but sounds great on the phone.)

It's likely you'll be forced at gunpoint to do an animatic sooner or later. There's nothing you can do about it. When it happens, just smile—no sudden movements—just smile, do the animatic, and back slowly out of the room, hands held up, palms out.

Simply get it over with. Someone once told me, "When you have to eat a turd, don't nibble."

FINDING THE RIGHT DIRECTOR

Involve your producer as early in the process as you can.

As the writer or art director on a TV commercial, you will be in charge of its creative direction all along the way. But you will have an ally to help bring your idea to the screen—the producer. Together, the three of you will see the commercial through from beginning to end.

Among many other duties, the agency's producer is in charge of the search for directors, bidding the job, arranging the casting sessions, staying on top of the budget, scheduling the shoot, researching special effects or stock footage, licensing the music, and knowing the bars where skinny creative people with cell phones and storyboards won't get beat up.

The good ones have the soul of a creative person and are conversant in both the technical and conceptual side of TV commercials. Get them on board early. Fill them in on the strategy as well as the concept. Tell them your vision for the spot—the tone, the look, the feeling you're trying to achieve. They'll need all this information when they set out to help you find the right director.

Make a thorough director search.

Some producers don't look further than the current A-list directors. The A-list is fine; you have to be good to be on it. But dig deeper. Many of Nike's best commercials were shot by unknowns discovered by the agency. Unknowns aren't just cheaper, they're hungrier. They bring a lot to the commercial.

As you look at a reel, try to see the original storyboard the director was working from.

You may be able to start *seeing* what he is bringing to the spot. But base your judgment on the film, not the concepts. (One way to do this is to review reels with the sound off.)

Pay attention to all the production values, the details—the set design, the props, the lighting. Are there innovative camera angles, moves, or lenses? Does the director shoot well outdoors, or is he better in the studio? Does the visual style enhance the concept? Are the performances good? Remember, all these details are the domain of the director.

Some directors just do funny better than others.

If you're doing a funny spot, look for the best comedy director. Note also that there are different kinds of funny—dark, broad, light, warm, frenetic. Look for these nuances in the reels and match the tone of your spot with the director who seems to handle your kind of material best.

This frame from an Alaska Airlines commercial (Fig. 5.10) is, unmistakably, one of director Joe Sedelmaier's spots. Sedelmaier invented this look—a world of puffy businessmen, pallid losers, and glassy-eyed corporate victims. Today, there are many other great directors. Choosing exactly the right one takes time.

Sell the director on your idea the same way you pitched it to the client.

You have one shot to get a good director excited about your spot. So don't just get them on the phone and walk them through the board.

Figure 5.10   Director Joe Sedelmaier invented this look. During the 1980s, there was Joe, and then there was everybody else.

Tell them about the client's marketing problem, how you came up with the idea, and what the competition is doing. Get them *into* it.

It doesn't hurt to tell the director which spots on his reel intrigued you. This isn't for the purpose of brownnosing either; it's just a good way to talk about intangibles with an artist. It helps when you can tell an architect, "You know that house you did on the lake? Yeah, we're thinking about something like that, only different."

Sell your idea. Remember, every morning at 10, the FedEx person delivers a cartload of storyboards to directors everywhere. It's likely you're competing with a lot of other great boards.

Give your director everything you can to describe your vision of the finished commercial.

After you get off the phone, write a short, descriptive essay on your spot describing how you see the commercial playing in your head.

Tell the director what you know about the target audience. Describe the characters. The set. The music you hear. What famous movie is it like? Do you have a feel for the look of the film, its palette of colors? Tear some photos from a magazine and send them along with the written description. The more you can give the director up front, the better.

- - -

CASTING YOUR COMMERCIAL

Casting the actors is the single most important decision you make during a commercial production.

It can be a long, boring process, and I often think untangling coat hangers is more fun; but stay vigilant. It will pay off.

A casting house (working from specs you provide) will call in a hundred or so actors and actresses and tape them as they read or play out a part. This tape is sent to your agency, where you and your partners pick out the ones you want to see again in person, or call back. In the callback session, you and the director see the actors perform live, see how well they take direction, and then make your final picks.

Piece of advice #1: Cast against grain.

Just because your board says "Businessman walks into room," you don't have to cast a trim, well-dressed yuppie. Go outside the box. Get strange. Not so strange that it detracts from the message, but cast somebody who isn't a Ken or Barbie. (Personally, I find that perfect-looking people disrupt a commercial even more than odd-balls. Whenever somebody who looks too good is talking to me, I barely hear what they're saying. I'm too busy thinking about how much I'd like to muss up their hair.)

For his famous Wendy's commercial (Fig. 5.11), writer Cliff Freeman could have cast a quiet little victim of a lady. Instead, he cast a charming loudmouth named Clara Peller. In the spot, Ms. Peller, disgusted with the small serving of meat on her bun, bellowed "Where's the beef?" and ended up on the cover of a hundred magazines.

Piece of advice #2: Cast the ones who can *act.*

Even if he doesn't look like the character you had in mind, book the best actor. If you book a bad one because he looks right, you'll regret it. Oh, how you'll regret it.

Figure 5.11   Clara Peller's diminutive stature and big voice helped move Wendy's "Where's the beef?" into the national conversation.

Let me put it this way. There are two kinds of Hell. There's "Original" and then there's "Extra Crispy." If you ever find yourself on the set of a very expensive commercial, at midnight, with a crew of 40 going into triple overtime, and you're about to do a 50th take trying to get a bad actor to read a line correctly, you will know what Extra Crispy Hell is. Book a good actor. You'll thank me for this later.

If you're going to use a celebrity, make sure the person is conceptually related to the benefit of your product.

It is not enough to film a Famous Guy. *("In between movies, I rely on one brand of rash cream.")* There is no such thing as borrowed interest.

Use your celebrity in an unusual way. Example: Dennis Hopper (known for his insane movie characters) became a deranged ex-referee, stalking the locker rooms to sniff Nike shoes worn by popular players.

Perhaps a good way to determine if a TV spot featuring a star is working is to make sure the commercial is entertaining even without the marquee name. If it is, you might be onto something. Remember, a star isn't a concept. Only an executional technique.

If you do go with a celeb, always send your idea to his agent before the client meeting to check on the star's willingness, cost, and availability. You don't want to write checks the client can't cash.

One last caveat. It doesn't happen very often, but celebrities have a way of turning up in hotel rooms with persons of questionable character, doubtful employment, and large Ziploc baggies of "Peruvian Marching Powder" tucked into their orange vinyl boots. Are you willing to bet a client's financial future that your superstar won't end up manufacturing license plates?

Don't put off casting the voice-over.

Do the same things you'd do in radio. Write out your casting specs. Be articulate; specify age, tone, attitude. And then fling them to agents far and wide. At the better ad agencies, listening to a hundred or so voices is baseline.

Listen to them all and make your shortlist. Start putting them up against the picture as soon as you can. How does each voice marry with the film?

The casting session: one last chance to improve your copy.

During the casting sessions, you'll have your first opportunity to hear somebody read your copy aloud. Now's your chance to listen for any stumbling blocks and take measures to correct them. Does the copy sound natural? Does it help advance the story? Use the casting sessions as an opportunity to perfect the copy. Then get it approved *before* the shoot.

THE SHOOT

The preproduction meeting is all-important. Be ready for it.

During the meeting, pay attention. It's the last calm hour before it really hits the fan.

At the prepro meeting, you, the account execs, the director, and the client will all sign off on every detail of the shoot. Mistakes and oversights at this meeting are bad. By the time they're discovered, the cameras are rolling, crews are on payroll, and time has run out. So pay attention.

Before you arrive at the prepro, however, you should be in agreement with your director on the broad strokes. You don't want the client diddling around with your shooting board this late in the game. So sit down with the director beforehand and go through every part of your spot. With tweezers.

What are the must-have master shots? What close-ups are absolutely necessary? Is this a dolly shot or is the camera locked down? What can you do with different camera angles or lenses to make it more filmic? What can you do with the lighting? Is there room enough on the product shot for the "super" (words that are superimposed over the picture)?

When you answer all the questions, go over it again.

Remember, aside from having to sit through the Ice Capades, there is nothing quite so horrifying as the discovery of a huge problem with your commercial after you're on the set.

"Compromise makes a great umbrella, but a bad roof."

In the prepro meeting, the client may bring up a problem with a particular scene. He may want it shot one way and you, another. Agreeing to shoot it two ways is a mistake.

It's unfair to saddle your director with more work because you can't make a decision. Adding an extra scene eats into the time he's allotted to shoot everything else. Shoots are crazy enough. Don't add work. Make a decision now and get ready to live with it.

When you're on the shoot, pay attention to your producer.

Television shoots are month-long periods of insanity. The only person who really knows what's going on is your producer. She's your only lifeline to reality. She knows the deadlines. She knows the budgets.

So, if your producer says you need to be somewhere at a certain time, be there. If she says she needs you to make a decision, make it. A shoot is no place to be lazy or sloppy. You will have your entire married life to lie around on the couch and put things off.

Talk to actors only through your director.

If you have something you want to tell the actor during the shoot, some new idea or a different way to read a line, tell it to your producer. Don't talk to actors directly. I did this once and got in trouble. Big trouble. Maybe you remember my face on the cover of *Big Trouble* magazine that month. Talking to the actors directly ticks directors off and rightfully so. *One* person needs to be directing the shoot. This is probably why they're called "directors." Just tell your idea to the producer and they'll find the right time for you to bring it up with the director.

A good director will usually get the actor to do just what you want—one way or the other. Which reminds me of a story Tom Monahan told me.

Young guy on the set of a commercial has a problem with the way the actor is reading a line. He follows protocol and approaches his CD with his concerns. The CD goes over to huddle with the producer, then the three of them go over to the director. "See, we'd like the actor to say the line with more force, but not in the *first* half of the line. Can he just look up from the table, and then say the line, but with not so much *punch* in the first half, but more in the *second* half?"

Director walks over to the actor and tells him, "Act better."

Speak up when you disagree with the director.

Sometimes the director will want to do something you're dead set against. What usually happens is that he's trying to stretch himself artistically (not a bad thing in itself), but in the process compromises the clarity of your message. The film starts to get too precious or overly artsy or "deep" or any number of affectations. If this happens, huddle up with your producer. Don't be shy. Be diplomatic, yes, but don't be shy. Speak up when you disagree. Some directors can be intimidating personalities; in their business, sometimes you have to be. But the director's job is to bring your selling message to life, not to bury it.

Okay, another story. A young writer is in LA on his first shoot. The director on the job happens to be the most respected and most mercurial auteur in the world, notorious for outbursts at crew and agency people alike. The writer, unaware of his director's eccentricities, blithely strolls up to him and speaks his mind about an idea for framing the next shot.

The cobra looks down at the mouse and says, "What is it you do?" Kid says, "I'm the copywriter."

"You're the *writer?*" The cobra calmly asks him to look through the camera, hissing, "Do you see any *words* in there?"

The kid looks and says no.

"NO? THEN GET THE #1@*!# OUTTA HERE!"

Ideally, the best spots are done in a collaborative atmosphere. Give and take, both ways.

Stay loose during the shoot. Be prepared to try anything.

Even if someone has an idea that's different from what's been boarded, be open to it. Production is a constantly evolving series of decisions, second-guesses, heart attacks, 1 A.M. phone calls, and poolside arguments. Be open to anything. Everything changes once the camera begins to roll. And then everything changes again at editing. It's great to have different things to experiment with. Get the storyboard in the can, then go for glory.

Keep thinking about alternate lines for the actors to read.

As you see the action unfolding during the shoot, you may see possibilities you couldn't when you were coming up with the idea. Try to determine if there are any last-minute improvements on the script you can feed to the director. Get the approved board in the can, but keep your wheels turning even as the camera rolls.

POSTPRODUCTION

Learn who the great editors are.

A great editor can take the same footage as a so-so editor and make an incredible difference. I've had commercials literally *saved* by good editing.

Familiarize yourself with the television editors out there, just as you keep up with who the good directors are. Ask your producers to feed your Rolodex with names of good new editors. Editors have reels just like directors do. Some are great comedy editors, some are better at music-video executions, and some are superb storytellers.

Send your editor the shooting boards as early in the process as you can. Their job is to tell a story with film. If your board lacks some key transitional scene, a sharp editor may be able to spot it.

There's another way to go. Let the director do it. Not many will offer to do a "director's cut," but if yours does, you may want to take him or her up on it.

Music is everything.

The wrong music can wreck a great spot just as surely as the right score can move a so-so spot onto the A-list. Give a lot of thought early on to the kind of music your commercial needs. Or if it needs any music at all.

Send your storyboards to the music house before you begin shooting. Most places will send back a "concept reel" with swatches of music in different styles, one of which might be just right for your spot. Other houses are willing to begin actually scoring tracks before you shoot, tracks you may want to use early in the editing process.

Don't settle for the first thing that seems to work. Keep putting different music up against the picture as long as the deadline will allow. And don't fall in love with any song your editor swipes off a CD. You can't "borrow" it, and any legal variation of it that you do in a final score will be so different from the original, what you liked about it will be long gone. To that end, take care when presenting a rough cut to a client. Make it clear that the music they're hearing now won't be on the final version.

Your opinions on the music will probably change as you see the spot evolve. Keep thinking about it all along the way. Involve your music house. Take their suggestions. Give them yours.

Pay close attention during the mix.

When you're at the final mix (where all the elements are put together), I suggest you mix key sound effects a teeny bit louder than the rest of the track. Play your finished spot back through the worst speakers you can find and make sure any sound effect that's *conceptually* important is audible.

Also, if your music company is doing the final mix, make sure they don't inadvertently let their music overpower the voice-over. It's understandable if they concentrate on making the music sound great. But you've got to keep the entire track in mind. Make sure you can understand every *word* of voice-over and dialogue.

Prepare a special cassette for the client presentation.

When preparing the presentation cassette for the client, get rid of the "slate" and "color bars" and record the spot twice, back to back. The client's going to want to see it at least twice anyway to form initial impressions. Save yourself the trouble of bending over to dink around with REV and FF buttons while the client has to look at your butt.

Keep your own "D-1" cassette.

As of this writing, D-1 is the best digital format available for storing video footage. It's like keeping your own master reel of your spots. After each final session, give your D-1 to your producer and ask if he or she can have your new spot added to it. It's something you'll be glad to have one day when you need to put together your reel in a big hurry.

Edit your TV reel like you would a TV spot.

When you're getting your reel together for an interview, don't just throw it together. Edit your reel on paper first. Then put together a few practice reels. Open strong. End strong.

But in the middle, pay attention to the flow. See what follows what. It's very much like editing scenes within a commercial. Certain things just look better in the right place. Make sure you mix up the genres—follow a talking spot with a musically driven one, a big production with a tabletop spot. You get the idea. You'll be surprised how some thoughtful editing can add flow and punch to your reel.

Figure 6.1 Everybody fights to get on a TV account. Everybody wants to do the color magazine spreads. And then there's radio.

6

Radio Is Hell.
But It's a Dry Heat.

*Some advice on working
in a tough medium*

IT IS ONE OF THE GREAT MYSTERIES of advertising. Most radio is, well, it's not very good.

Over the years, I've judged many awards shows. In every show I can remember, the judges loved poring over the print. Looking at the TV was fun. But when the time came to sit down and listen to several hours of radio commercials, the room thinned out. Nobody wanted to do it.

I wish I knew why. I don't. Radio scares me, too. But it pays to learn to do it as well as you can. Not many people know how. Ed McCabe advised young writers, "Quick, do something good on radio before someone catches on and makes it as difficult as it is everywhere else."

Done well, it's an incredibly powerful medium. Copywriter Tom VanSteenhoven wrote a good line about great radio. "It goes in one ear . . . and stays there."

WRITING THE COMMERCIAL

Radio is visual.

It's a tired old cliché, but there's truth in it. Radio has been called "theater of the mind." The good commercials out there capitalize on this fact. In radio you can do things you can't in any other medium.

You can make the listener see the impossible image of a cactus-man in a werewolf mask pour through the keyhole and eat your cat. (Actually, I *did* see this once in college, but I . . . never mind.)

The point is, in radio the canvas is large, stretching off in every direction. Use it.

"Sometimes I've believed as many as six impossible things before breakfast." —Lewis Carroll

Cover the wall with scripts.

When you're working in radio, come up with a lot of ideas, just like you do when you write for print.

There is no law that says radio has to be funny.

I can assure you that humor is the first fork in the road taken by every copywriter in the nation on every radio job they get. I don't blame them. It's fun to laugh and radio seems to beg for it.

But do the math. According to the American Association of Advertising Agencies, there are 13,690 U.S. agencies as of this writing. Even if they're all producing just one radio spot a week, by the end of the year you're looking at nearly three quarters of a million commercials all vying to be the funniest. I don't like the odds.

If you want to stand out in this medium, try something other than humor. It may not work, but you should at least try.

Here's an example. It's a very straightforward, very sober-minded radio spot for a bank, written by my friends Phil Hanft and Pat Burnham when they were at Fallon McElligott. I doubt this spot (or any of the following commercials) will come off as well on paper as they do on the radio. Broadcast advertising rarely makes the translation to print very gracefully. On this page you can't hear the nostalgic instrumental rendition of "Stand By Me" playing quietly underneath this 90-second script. And you can't hear the candor and honesty in the actor's voice.

> MAN: I guess you could say I'm kinda slow to do the big things in life. I mean, there's some stuff I think we'd all agree you just shouldn't rush into. Like buying a house. Took me a long time to do that. Some might say too long. Now when I tell friends who are younger about the benefits of buying a house, I can see that familiar doubt. That look behind the eyes that says "Yeah, I hear you and yeah I know you're right and that's true and I agree, but you know I can't tell you this because I know you won't understand, but it's a big deal and I'm just not sure it's going to go the same way for me as it did for you because I haven't done it." I guess somebody could say that's fear, but I don't think so. That's fear, like jumping off a building is courage. Forget that. All I can say now is what everybody said to me back then. It's the best thing to do. I did it. You should do it. 'Cept I would also add . . . I know how you feel right now. And it's okay.

> ANNCR VO: A reminder from First Tennessee that whatever stage of life you're in, it's far less difficult when you have money in the bank. First Tennessee. Member FDIC.

Maybe it's one of those you-had-be-there things, but this radio spot stands out in my mind as one of the best I've ever heard. Partly because of its incredible production values. And partly because it isn't another Yuk-Fest, Laff-A-Minit radio script cranked out by a frustrated stand-up comedian doing time in an ad agency until his agent calls. It was real.

Make sure your radio spot is important or scary or funny or interesting within the first five seconds.

Your spot just interrupted your listener's music. It's like interrupting people having sex. If you're going to lean in the bedroom door to say something, make it good: "Hey, your car's on fire."

If your spot's not interrupting music, it's probably following on the heels of a bad commercial. Your listener is already bored. There's no reason for him to believe your commercial's going to be any better. Not a good time to bet on a slow build.

Also, awards-show judges, like consumers, are *very* harsh. They'll grumble "fast forward" in about five seconds if your spot isn't striking their fancy.

The following spot has an interesting opening line. (I include it for more reasons than just the setup: It's a simple premise, 130 words long, with no sound effects, and it entertains the whole way through.) It's a British spot and it may help to hear it read with a droll English accent.

> MALE VO: My life. By an ordinary HP-grade battery.
>
> Monday. Bought by the Snoads of Jackson Road, Balham. Placed in their [flashlight]. At last. A career.
>
> Tuesday. How can I describe the cupboard under the stairs? After much thought, I've come up with . . . "dark."
>
> Wednesday. The Snoad's hamster goes walkabout. After nearly five hours of continuous blazing torchlight, we track it down on Clapham Common.
>
> Thursday. Oh dear. I'm dead. They swapped me for Duracell. It can power a [flashlight] non-stop for 39 hours. Which is nearly a full eight hamsters.
>
> Friday. How can I describe the [garbage can]? After much thought, I've come up with . . . "rank." Still, I've led an interesting life. It's just been a bit . . . "short."
>
> ANNOUNCER: Duracell. No ordinary battery looks like it. Or lasts like it.

Funny isn't enough. You must have an idea.

Should you do something humorous, don't mistake a good joke for a good idea. Funny is fine. But set out to be interesting first. You must have an idea.

Here's an example of an interesting premise, written by my friend Craig Weise.

> ANNCR: Recently, Jim Paul of Valley Olds-Pontiac-GMC was driving to work when . . . (MAN: "Gee, look at that.") . . . he noticed a large inflatable gorilla floating above another dealer-

ship. He'd noticed several of these inflatable devices floating above car dealerships lately and he asked himself some questions. Did anybody ever go into that dealership and say, "Great gorilla. Makes me feel like buying a car." Why don't other businesses use gorillas? Would people be more likely to buy, say, a new home with a gorilla tethered to the chimney? "Three bedrooms, two-and-a-half baths, sun porch . . . gorilla." Would people have more confidence in the doctors if a medical clinic featured a gorilla on the roof? Without car dealers, would there even *be* an inflatable gorilla business? Right then, Jim Paul made an important, courageous decision on behalf of his fine dealership. (MAN: "I don't think I'll get a gorilla.") Just 8 miles south of the Met Center on Cedar Avenue, Jim Paul's Valley Olds-Pontiac-GMC. A car dealership for the times.

Over lunch one day, Craig pointed out that there are no gags in this spot, no goofy-sounding voice-over. Just a guy reading about 160 words. And although radio is often described as a visual medium, Craig called this an example of radio as print. I think he's right. This commercial is simply an essay. Yet I think it's an incredibly funny spot. So did a lot of listeners. This commercial made a *bunch* of money for Mr. Paul.

Find your voice.

Imagine how a novelist's fingers must start to fly over the keys once she discovers her character. Finding your voice in radio can be just as liberating.

Think about *who* your character is. What's his take on your client's product or on the category? Is he thoughtful or sarcastic? Cynical or wry? Once you find this voice, you will see the material unfold before you, see all the possibilities for future executions, and your pen will start to move.

Some of the best radio out there is just one voice reading ten sentences. But it's that attitude the voice has, its take on the material that makes it so compelling.

I'm thinking of one campaign in particular: the long-running *Crain's New York Business* magazine campaign written by my friend, Dean Hacohen. There was no music. No sound effects. Just one guy talking slowly. And convincingly. A flat read with no ups and downs. Just a *guy*. Here's the script for one of the *Crain's* spots.

> ANNCR: Just off the boardwalk in Coney Island, you'll find the New York Aquarium. There, in a tank in the main lobby, swims one of the smallest, yet most vicious predators the world has ever known: the red piranha. With its razor-sharp teeth, this bloodthirsty creature can attack, decimate, and devour its unknowing prey in seconds. If you are an executive in the New York area, and feel you can stay safely ahead of your competitors without the information in *Crain's New York Business,* we strongly suggest you come down to the aquarium at feeding time for a demonstration.

Write radio sparely.

Unless your concept demands a lot of words and fast action, write sparely. This allows your voice talent to read your script slowly. Quietly. One word at a time.

You'll be surprised at how this kind of bare-bones execution *leaps* out of the radio. There is a remarkable power in silence. It is to radio what white space is to print. Silence enlarges the idea it surrounds.

But even if your idea isn't a bare-bones kind of idea, write sparely. There's nothing worse than showing up at the studio with a fat script. You'll be forced to edit under pressure.

If a 60-second spot is a house, a 30 is a tent.

Thirties are a different animal. If you think you're writing sparely for a 60-second commercial, for a 30 we're talking maybe 60 words. Thirties call for a different brand of thinking. It's a lot like writing a 10-second TV spot. If your 30 is to be a funny spot, the comedy has to be fast. A quick pie in the face.

Here's an example of a very simple premise that rolls itself out quickly.

> ANNOUNCER: We're here on the street getting consumer reaction to the leading brand of dog food.

VARIOUS VOICES ON STREET: Yelllllchh! Aaaarrrrrgh! Gross! This tastes awful!

ANNOUNCER: If you're presently a buyer of this brand, may we suggest Tuffy's dry dog food. Tuffy's is nutritionally complete and balanced and it has a taste your dog will love. And at a dollar less per bag, it comes with a price you can swallow.

VOICES ON STREET: Yellllch! Aaaarrrrrgh!

ANNOUNCER: Tuffy's. A doggone good dog food.

Get a stopwatch and time it.

Read it slowly while you do. Sometimes I'll find myself cheating the clock in order to convince myself there's time to include a favorite bit. I'll read it fast but pretend I'm reading it slowly. I know, it's pathetic, but it happens. Read your script s l o w l y.

If you're doing a dialogue, do it extremely well.

Write it exactly as people actually speak. This can be tough.

One of the problems you face with dialogue is weaving a sales message into the natural flow of conversation. "Can I have another one of those Flavor-rific® brownies, now with one-third larger chocolate bits, Mom?" Always hard. Better to let a straight voice-over do the heavy lifting.

Remember, just as the eye isn't fooled by cheap special effects, the ear picks up even slight divergences from real speech. Be careful with dialogue.

This next spot is a good example of dialogue and a personal favorite. It's written by London's Tim Delaney. (Again, if you can read this copy with an English accent, all the better.)

SFX: *Shop door with bell, opening and closing*

CUSTOMER (CLEARLY AN IDIOT): Morning, squire.

CLERK (PATIENT AND WISE): Morning, sire.

CUSTOMER: I'd like a videocaster, please.

CLERK: A video recorder. Any one in particular?

CUSTOMER: Well, I'd like to have some specifications . . .

CLERK: Yes?

CUSTOMER: . . . and functions. I *must* have some functions.

CLERK: I see. Did you have any model in mind?

CUSTOMER: Well, a friend mentioned the Airee-Keeri-Kabuki-uh-Kasumi-uh watchamacallit. You know, the Japanese one, the 2000. 'Cause I'm very technically minded, you see.

CLERK: I can see that.

CUSTOMER: So I want mine with all the little bits on it. All the Japanese bits. You know, the 2000.

CLERK: What system?

CUSTOMER: Uh, uh, well, electrical I think, because I'd like to be able to plug it into the television. You see, I've got a *Japanese* television.

CLERK: Have you?

CUSTOMER: Yeah, I thought you'd be impressed. Yeah, the 2000, the Oki-Koki 2000.

CLERK: Well, sir, there is *this* model.

CUSTOMER: Yeah, looks smart, yeah.

CLERK: Eight hours per cassette, *all* the functions that the others have, and I know this will be of interest. A lot of scientific research has gone into making it easy to operate . . .

CUSTOMER: Good, yeah.

CLERK: . . . even by a comp*lete* idiot like you.

CUSTOMER: Pardon?

CLERK: It's a Phillips.

CUSTOMER: Doesn't sound very Japanese.

CLERK: No, a Phirrips. I mean, a Phirrips. It's a Phirrips.

CUSTOMER: Yeah, it's a 2000, is it?

CLERK: Oh, in fact it's the 2022.

CUSTOMER: Hmmmm . . . no. Hasn't got enough knobs on it. Nope. What's that one over there?

CLERK: That's a washing machine.

CUSTOMER: Yeah? What? It's a Japanese? *(Fade-out)*

ANNCR VO: The VR 2022. Video you can understand. From Phirrips.

Read your radio out loud.

You'll hear things to improve that you won't pick up just by scanning the script. The written and spoken word are different. Make sure your writing sounds like everyday speech. Read it aloud.

Avoid the formula of "shtick—serious sales part—shtick reprise."

You've heard them. The spots begin with some comic situation tangentially related to the product benefit. Then, about 40 seconds into the spot, an announcer comes in to "get serious" and sell you something. After which there's a happy little visit back to the joke.

One of the problems with this structure is the ungraceful moment when the salesman in his plaid coat pops out of the closet. This shtick-sales-shtick structure can work, but make sure you don't jar your listeners too much when you switch over to sales mode.

Personally, I think it's better to construct a comic situation that you don't have to "leave" in order to come around to the sale. Here's a great example of premise flowing seamlessly into sale, written by Mike Renfro of The Richards Group.

MAN (IN A VERY STRAIGHTFORWARD, MONOTONE VOICE): Ever had the feeling when you're driving that idiots just seem to follow you wherever you go? Well, it's true. I should know. You see, I am an idiot and I've been assigned to you. Actually, I'm only one of three idiots assigned to you. We each work eight-hour shifts. This month, I happen to be on days. So it's my job to dog you relentlessly. Today, I might be the guy in the blue Nova who cuts you off. Tomorrow, the guy in the orange Pacer who runs a light. Next week, who knows? Which is why you might want to be certain you're properly insured. With me and my colleagues out here, you need to call Great American Insurance Company. They're a company that's been around since 1872. And since they don't cover guys like me, they can save good drivers money. Just tell 'em some idiot on the radio sent you.*

ANNOUNCER: Great American®. Call 1-800-555-XXXX

Make your spot entertaining all the way to the end, particularly when you get to the sell.

I've heard many radio spots that start out great, but when they get to the selling message, sputter out and fail. You can't just write off the sell as "the announcer stuff." It is part and parcel of the spot. It's the hardest part to make palatable but also the most important.

A humorous radio spot is like a good stand-up comedy routine. You need to open funny and end funny. And in the middle, you need to "pulse" the funny bits, to keep 'em coming. Do a funny line and then allow some breathing room, another funny bit, then more mortar, then another brick, mortar, brick, mortar. Actually, such a structure can serve a commercial of any tone—just keep reeling out something interesting every couple of feet.

This commercial from BBDO West sells all the way through. But the way it's written, you're entertained throughout. It's just one guy, a very straitlaced voice-over reading 189 words without a trace of irony.

ANNOUNCER: Fire ants are not lovable. People do not want fire-ant plush toys. They aren't cuddly. They don't do little tricks. They just bite you and leave red, stinging welts that make you want to cry. That's why they have to die. And they have to die right now. You don't want them to have a long, lingering illness. You want death. A quick, excruciating, see-you-in-hell kind of death. You don't want to lug a bag of chemicals and a garden hose around the yard. It takes too long. And baits can take up to a week. No, my friend, what you want is Ant-Stop Orthene Fire Ant Killer from Ortho. You put two teaspoons of Ant-Stop around the mound and you're done. You don't even water it in. The scout ants bring it back into the mound. And this is the really good part. Everybody dies. Even the queen. It's that fast.

*Used by permission of Great American Insurance Company, Cincinnati, Ohio.

And that's *good.* Because killing fire ants shouldn't be a full-time job. Even if it *is* pretty fun. Ant-Stop Orthene Fire-Ant Killer from Ortho. Kick fire-ant butt.

Once you get an idea you like, write the entire spot before you decide it doesn't work.

Tell your internal editor to put a sock in it. Just get that raw material on paper. You may find that in the writing you fix what was bothering you about the commercial.

Avoid the temptation to use any sort of brand name or other copyrighted material.

As an example, I once wrote a script where I referred to The Beatles. They weren't the focus of the spot; their name was used in an offhanded sort of aside. The spot was approved but one week before we recorded the script, the lawyers landed on it like a ton of hair spray and cell phones. When I tried to rewrite it, days after the original heat of the creative moment had cooled, I found myself unable to replace the line without repair marks showing.

Lesson: Don't even touch copyrighted stuff. Famous people, brand names, even dead guys who've been taking a dirt nap for 50 years—their lawyers are all still alive. Stay generic.

Don't do jingles.

Do I have to say this? Jingles are a boring, corny, horrible, and sad thing left over from Eisenhower's '50s—a time, actually, when *everything* was boring, corny, horrible, and sad. Avoid jingles as you would a poisonous toad. They are death.

─────

THE JOY OF SFX

A sound effect can lead to a concept.

It's an interesting place to start. Find a sound that has something to do with your product or category and play with it.

Here's an example of a sound effect, set inside a good comic premise, and used to great effect.

SFX: *Telephone ring*

MAN: Hello.

CALLER: Oh. I'm sorry. I was looking for another number.

MAN: 976-EDEN?

CALLER: Well, . . . yeah.

MAN: You got it.

CALLER: The flyer said to ask for Eve.

MAN: Yeah, well she's not here. I can help you.

CALLER: Oh, . . . no. That's okay, I'll just . . .

MAN: Hold on, hold on. Let me get the apple.

CALLER: The apple?

MAN: You ready? Here goes . . .

SFX: *Big juicy crunch of an apple*

CALLER: That's . . . you're eating an apple. That's the "little bit of paradise" you advertised?

MAN: Well, that's a "little *bite* of paradise." The printer made a mistake.

CALLER: I'm supposed to sit here and listen to you eat an apple?

MAN: Well, it *is* a Washington Apple.

SFX: *Crunch*

CALLER: Look, I'm not going to pay $3 a minute just to sit here while you . . .

MAN: Nice, big, Red Delicious Washington Apple.

SFX: *Crunch*

CALLER: . . . eat an apple. . . . It does sound good.

MAN: It's nice and crisp, you know.

CALLER: Sounds good.

MAN: Kinda sweet.

CALLER: Uh-huh.

MAN: Fresh.

CALLER: I shouldn't . . . this is silly . . .

SFX: *Crunch*

CALLER: What are you wearing?

MAN: Well, a flannel shirt and a paisley ascot.

CALLER: Oh. Describe the apple again.

MAN: Mmmmm-hmmmm.

ANNOUNCER: Washington Apple.

SFX: *Crunch*

ANNOUNCER: They're as good as you've heard.

Don't overdo sound effects.

Sound effects can be great tools for radio. They can help tell a story. They can *be* the story. But don't overuse them or expect them to do things they can't.

Since 90 percent of radio listening is done in the car (to and from work, during what media buyers call "drive time"), minute subtleties are going to be lost. The buttoning of a shirt does indeed make a sound, but it probably isn't enough to communicate somebody getting dressed.

My friend, Mike Lescarbeau, says any day now he expects a client to ask him to open a radio spot with "the sound effect of somebody getting a great value."

Don't waste time explaining things.

We hear the sound effect of a knock at the door. Does the next line really have to be "Hey, someone's at the door"? No. Let the sound effects tell your story for you. People are smart. They'll fill in the blanks if you provide the structure.

Avoid cacophony.

You might as well learn now you can't put sirens in a radio spot. At least not in my market. I can see why. It confuses drivers. They hear a siren sound effect on their radio and pull over to let an ice cream truck pass by.

While we're on the subject of irritating noises, keep any kind of cacophony out of your spot. That includes yelling, even comedic yelling. It grates on the listener. Especially on the third and fourth airing.

I've always thought of radio as the best medium to target carpenters. These guys have their radios on all day. They're not just going to hear your spot, they're going to hear the entire radio *buy*. One carpenter told me he actually changes stations to avoid hearing an irritating spot played over and over again.

Keep this in mind when you write. Remember, carpenters have hammers.

Have your sound effects ready and waiting for you on recording day.

Call the studio a week or two before you record and ask them if they can put together a reel of any sound effects you need. If you're using needle-drop (stock) music, describe what you have in mind and see if they can put together a short reel. Listen to it before the session. If it isn't right, politely ask for more.

———

CASTING: BORING, TEDIOUS, ESSENTIAL

Cast and cast and cast.

Casting is everything. In radio, the voice-over you choose is the star, the wardrobe, the set design, everything all rolled into one. It's the most important decision you make during production.

Start casting as soon as possible. Send your script to as many casting houses in as many major cities as you can. I strongly suggest two of those cities be Los Angeles and New York.

Along with the scripts, send your casting specs: some description of the quality of voice you have in mind. If it's relevant, use the name of some Hollywood star to give the casting folks a sense of the kind of voice you have in mind.

About a week later, the tapes will begin to roll in. Listen to all of them (at my agency, 100 auditions for one voice is average). Make your selections and then ask your producer if he or she will kindly pull those selects and put them on one tape. Hearing a shortlist of the better voices back-to-back allows you to zero in on those nuances that can make a real difference. (One voice may come from New York, another Los Angeles. It doesn't matter; you can digitally patch them into your local recording studio.)

Your third tape and final shortlist should be your top three. By then you should be able to pick your favorite. You'll also have a second and third choice to go back to if your client has a problem with the one you like.

One last note: Consider using the voice of just "some guy"—a friend, the babysitter, or somebody in the media department. A modicum of talent is necessary, but it can work.

For those first cattle calls, ask your producer to tell the casting houses, "One take per talent."

Actors and actresses understandably want to win the part. So they'll often read your script three or four different ways. But an actor either has the pipes for a certain part or he doesn't. Having to listen to each actor read a script four different ways adds hours to the casting process with no benefit to you. Tell them one take per talent, please.

Don't choose a popular voice-over.

Every year, a hot new voice becomes wildly popular and turns up in just about every radio and TV spot. If you choose a popular voice-over, he may not be competing with himself in your local market, but I offer this advice, self-serving as it is: Come awards-show time, the judges will hear this voice-over compete with himself. No matter how great your spot is, it will sound like all the others.

As you listen to the casting tapes, keep an open mind about that voice you're looking for.

You may discover someone who brings a whole new approach to your script. Sometimes it comes from an ad-lib or from an actor who doesn't understand the soul of the spot. These fresh approaches to your material may open up new possibilities on how you might produce the final commercial.

Rewrite based on what you learn from the casting tapes.

You'll have one last chance to make your radio spot better. When the casting tapes roll in and you're listening to the actors read your lines, keep an ear cocked for those sentences where the actors stumble.

If more than one actor has a problem with a line, it's likely it's the line that's the problem, not the actors.

Listen for the general flow. Is it entertaining in the first ten seconds? In the second ten? The last? Are you saying the same thing twice? Are you saying the same thing twice? If you can take something out, do it now. It's your last chance to make a change and have the client sign off before you go into the studio.

A friend of mine, Glenn Gill, suggests listening to casting tapes on your car's tape deck as you go to work. It's a great way to get something done during downtime, and the voices that stand out on your car radio may well do the same on everybody else's one day.

Keep a file on your favorite actors and actresses. You'll need it.

There are situations when you don't have time to cast. The job comes in and has to be on the air in 48 hours. This is when a list of your favorite voice-overs comes in very handy.

When you don't have any time to cast, write for an actor or actress you know. Somebody you've worked with before and had success with. Pick some favorite voices out of your file and start thinking. "What could I do with her voice? What funny thing could he do for this client?" It's a great way to kick-start the concept motor, and you have some comfort knowing that whatever you come up with, your voice-over will be just right for the job.

Sometimes the best way to present a spot is to do a demo.

Ask your producer if there's a couple hundred in the budget you could use for this purpose. If your spot depends on the unique presentation of a particular actor's voice, this may be the way to go.

PRODUCING A RADIO COMMERCIAL

Production is where 90 percent of all radio spots fail.

Learn how and learn well all the elements of production. For some reason I don't understand, radio is an all-or-nothing medium. It works or it doesn't. There is no in between.

Copywriter Tom Monahan on radio:

> In radio, there's simply no place to hide anything. No place for the mistakes, the poor judgment, the weaknesses. Everything is right there in front for all 30 or 60 seconds. Everything must be good for the spot to be good. The concept, copy, casting, acting, production—everything. One of them goes wrong, sorry, but it's tune-out time.[1]

So, start with a good idea. Craft it into a great script. Congratulations, you are 10 percent of the way there.

Develop a good working relationship with a local audio engineer.

My friend, copywriter Phil Hanft, reminded me of the importance of finding a good recording engineer in your town—a technician with a great ear who will add to the process. One who understands timing, the importance of the right sound effects and the right music. Not someone who wants to get you in and out as fast as possible or someone who agrees with everything you do. As William Wrigley Jr. said, "When two people in business always agree, one of them is unnecessary."

Book enough time in the studio.

With all the work you've put into writing the spot, it would be a shame to have to throw it together. It's better to overbook time than to underbook it.

Keep the studio entourage to a minimum.

Try to produce your spot alone. Well, just you and the engineer, I mean. No clients. No account executives. Not that they're bad people and you, you alone, are a Radio God. It's just that large crowds bring tension into those small rooms. Your spot will have more focus if it isn't produced by a committee of six.

Provide your talent with scripts that are easy to read.

Unless your actor really needs to see the cues of sound effects (or the lines of another actor), cut out everything except what he has to read. Set the type in something like 14-point, and double-space it (so there's room to scribble in any last-minute changes).

Don't worry about proper punctuation. Write for the flow of speech. And underline or italicize words you know you want the voice-over to hit. But don't OVERdo it <u>or</u> your *final* read IS <u>going</u> *to* SUCK.

Also, come to the session prepared to cut certain lines in the event your script runs long. Know in advance what to cut or you'll find yourself rewriting under pressure at the studio. Not good.

When you're in the recording studio, tell the voice-over to read it straight.

Most of them have been trained by years of copywriters telling them to "put a *smile* in your voice" or to hit the word "tomorrow" in the line "So come on in *tomorrow*." People don't talk like that. Have your voice-over talk like you talk. I find a flat read is best.

When directing talent, be precise.

My engineer friend Andre Bergeron says he often sees writers directing with flabby, inarticulate language that leaves the talent clueless and uncomfortable. "Can you make that read more ... more *green?*"

Try not to be so ... so ... what's the word ... irritating.

My advice: For the first few takes, let the talent read it the way she wants. Some of them are very experienced. If your script is great, she may pick up on what you want right at the outset. If she doesn't, fine; you've involved the talent up front and now you both have a baseline from which to work.

Also, don't wear out your talent by making them start from the top for every take. If you've got a good opening on tape, do what's called a "pickup" and start the read further into the script. Then do a quick edit to see if it cuts together. It usually does.

Don't let the talent steamroll you.

If you're a young writer on your first studio session, let your engineer in on this fact, but not the talent. The engineer, if he's a good soul, will show you the ropes and teach what you need to know. But if the voice-over catches a whiff of "junior meat" in the studio, they'll take over the session, particularly if you're working with some of the higher-priced Hollywood or New York talent. Don't let it happen.

TV shoots are controlled by the director. Radio, by the writer. Stay in charge of the room. Give and take is fine, but ultimately you're the one who has to show up back at the agency with a cassette. If you're new to the business, it's probably not a bad idea to ask a senior writer if you can observe a few recording sessions before you tackle one alone.

Don't be afraid to stray from the script.

It's just the architecture. Get the client-approved script in the can, but if something else seems to be working, explore it. Record those other ideas and come back to experiment with them later.

Spread your production over a couple of days.

Record voices on the first day, review all the takes, and make your selections of the best tracks. Maybe get a rough cut done. But save the music, sound effects, and final mix for the next day. That second day gives you a chance to react to your spot more objectively.

Don't overproduce.

I've seen it happen a million times. You get into that tiny room with all the knobs and buttons. You drink too much coffee. You start messing with the "s" on the end of the word "prices," borrowing the "s" from take 17 and putting it on "price" from 22. You start taking a breath out here and adding it there. By the time you're done, you have a slick, surgically perfect piece of rubbish that sounds as natural as Pat Nixon.

When painting a picture, never put your nose closer than six inches to the canvas.

If your client can afford it, always produce one more radio spot than you need.

It's the darnedest thing. But the script you thought was the hilarious one turns out to be the least funny. It happens every time I go into the studio. One or two spots are simply going to be better than the others. The more you have to choose from, the better.

One way to get a few more spots out of the session is to record your alternate scripts at what they call "demo" rates and then upgrade the talent (pay the full rate) if the client approves the commercials.

Send the client a cassette for approval. Don't phone it in.

If you have an out-of-town client, build an extra day into the production schedule so you can overnight the finished commercial to them. You don't want clients approving radio spots over the phone. Over the phone, they can't hear the subtleties of the mix, they can't hear the timing, they can't hear anything. It's like describing Disneyland over the phone to your kids and expecting them to have a good time. "Yeah, and you should see Mickey and Goofy. They walked right *by* me here, just a minute ago. Isn't this *fun?*"

Keep a digital master of every spot you record.

Bring a digital audiotape to each mix session and compile your own master reel. It beats having a hundred cassettes clutter up your office. And when you need to send out a reel, you can put your best five or six spots on a compact disc. It doesn't cost a lot and it looks cool.

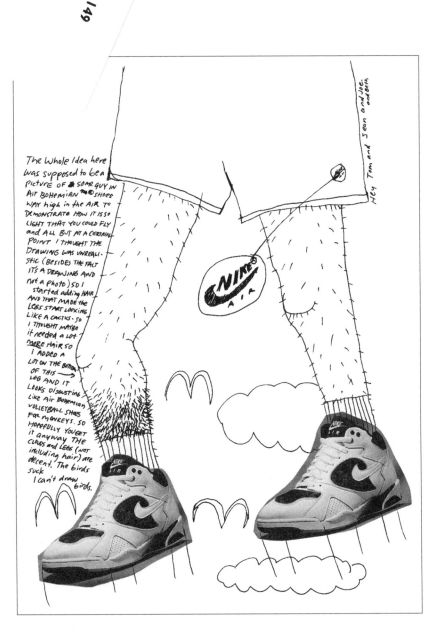

The Whole Idea here was supposed to be a picture of a some guy in AIR BOHEMIAN shoes way high in the AIR to Demonstrate how it is so light that you could fly and all. but at a certain point I thought the drawing was unrealistic (besides the fact it's a drawing and not a photo) so I started adding HAIR AND THAT MADE the LEGS START LOOKING LIKE A CACTUS. so I thought maybe it needed a lot more HAIR so I added a lot on the bottom of this → LEG AND IT LOOKS disgusting Like Air Bohemian VOLLEYBALL SHOES FOR MONKEYS. so hopefully you get it anyway THE CLOUDS and LEGS (not including hair) are decent. The birds suck I can't draw birds.

HEY Tom and Sean and Joe. and Seth

Figure 7.1   An author of a book on creativity wrote: "An idea is nothing more or less than a new combination of old elements." And then there's this.

7

"Toto, I Have a Feeling We're Not in McCann-Erickson Anymore."

Working out past the edge

PICASSO PROBABLY LEARNED TO DRAW a realistic head before he began putting both eyes on the same side of the nose.

Getting the eyes in the right place has been the subject of the first chapters of this book. Once you learn how, it's time to go farther out. So take everything I've said so far and just chuck it. Every rule, every guideline, just give 'em the old heave-ho.

Let's assume you know how to sell a vacuum cleaner in a small-space ad with a well-crafted headline. Let's assume you know how to put a great visual idea on paper and how to come up with the sort of idea that makes colleagues who see it go, "Hey, great ad."

Doyle Dane art director Helmut Krone had this to say on the subject:*

If people tell you, "That's up to your usual great standard," then you know you haven't done it. "New" is when you've never seen before

---

*Reprinted with permission from the Oct. 14, 1968, issue of *Advertising Age*. Copyright, Crain Communications Inc. 1968.

what you've just put on a piece of paper. You haven't seen it before and nobody else in the world has ever seen it. . . . It's not related to anything that you've seen before in your life. And it's very hard to judge the value of it. You distrust it, and everybody distrusts it. And very often, it's somebody else who has to tell you that the thing has merit, because you have no frame of reference.[1]

There's going to come a point in your job when the compasses don't work. When you're so far out there that up ceases to be up, west isn't west, and "Hey, great ad" is replaced with "What the hell is this?" Perhaps this is how the lay of the land looked when my friends Jelly Helm and Jamie Barrett at Wieden & Kennedy came up with this ad for Nike (Fig. 7.2).

What "rules," what advice in this book could possibly have led a creative team to come up with this? None that I can think of. There is no bridge across some chasms. Only great leaps of imagination can make it across. We're not talking about small increments of experimental thinking anymore, or reformulations or permutations, but entire new languages. New ways of looking at things. Or what Tom Wolfe called "pushing the outside of the envelope."[2]

Once you've learned to draw a realistic head, this creative outland is where you're going to need to go. This point is important enough that I've devoted this whole, albeit short, chapter to it. The last rule is this: Once you've learned the rules, throw them out.

Any further advice I give at this point is counterproductive to the creative process. It's as if I'm looking over artist Jackson Pollack's shoulder saying, "I think you need another splat of blue over there."

But even out in deep space, there is one rule you are obliged to obey. You must be relevant.

You're never going to get so far out there that you can dare not to be relevant to your audience. No matter how creative you think an idea is, if it has no meaning to your audience, you don't have an ad. You may have art. But you don't have an ad.

"LOVE, HONOR, AND OBEY YOUR HUNCHES."
—LEO BURNETT

Bernbach said, "Execution becomes content in a work of genius."

It is never more true than out here, where concepts can some-

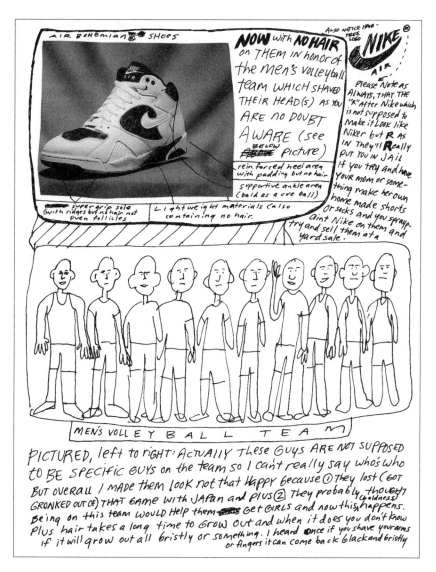

Figure 7.2   *Nobody's broken more rules than Nike.*

times be *all* execution without the traditional sales message. To have such an execution succeed, you're going to need to know your customer better than the competition does. You're going to need to know what he likes, how he thinks, and how he moves through his world. If your commercial reflects these inner realities you'll succeed, because your viewer's going to think, "This company knows me."

Here's a good example of how keen awareness of the customer, an intuition, and incredible production values colluded to make advertising history.

Consider the following TV script. There is no music.

> BANKER: "There's a lot of paperwork here. There's always paperwork when you buy a house. First one says that you lose the house if you don't make your payments. You probably don't want to think about that but . . . you do have to sign it. Next says the property is insured for the amount of the note. And you sign that in the lower left corner. This pretty much says that nobody's got a gun to your head . . . that you're entering the agreement freely. Next is the house is free of termites. Last one says that the house will be your primary residence and that you won't be relying on rental income to make the payments. I hope you brought your checkbook. This is the fun part. I say that all the time though most people don't think so. (*Chuckle*)"

This was one of the famous TV spots for John Hancock Financial Services that swept every awards show around 1986. Accompanying this script were images of a young married couple buying their first house as they sat in front of a loan officer's desk. The scenes were intercut with quick shots of type listing different investment services offered by John Hancock.

I'm sure that on paper, the board looked a little flat. In fact, it probably *still* looks flat here. But this is precisely my point. In the hands of a director other than Joe Pytka or a creative team less seasoned than Bill Heater and Don Easdon, this little vignette *could* have been flat.

But what made this storyboard work was the gut feeling the creative team had for the cotton-mouthed, shallow-breathing tension some people have when parting with a great deal of money. They successfully brought the full force of this emotion alive and kicking onto the TV screen.

There were no special effects, no comic exaggerations, or any other device I may have touched on in this book. Just an intuition two guys had, successfully transferred to ¾-inch tape.

Mark Fenske told me, "You cannot logic your way to an audience's heart." People are not rational. We like to think we are, but we're not. If you look unflinchingly at your own behavior, you may agree that few of the things you do, you do for purely rational reasons. Consumers, being people, are no different. Most people buy things for emotional reasons and then, after the fact, figure out a logical explanation for their purchase decision.

So that's the other piece of advice: Trust your intuitions. Trust your feelings. As you try to figure out what would persuade somebody to buy your product, consider what would make you buy it. Dig inside. If you have to, write the damn strategy after you do the ad. Forget about the stinkin' focus groups and explore the feelings you have about the product.

If an idea based on these feelings makes sense to you, it will probably make sense to others. Someone once told me that the things about myself that are the most personal are also the most universal. Trust your instincts. They are valid.

BUILD A SMALL, COZY FIRE WITH THE RULE BOOKS. START WITH THIS ONE.

It has been said there are no new ideas. Picasso himself said, "All art is theft." Historian Will Durant wrote, "Nothing is new except arrangement."

I've used these statements myself to defend ads I've written. Ads that were sound and good, but weren't way out there and should have been. I think I was wrong. Instead, I think it's better to believe there really are whole new ways of communicating, ways that nobody has discovered yet. I urge you to look for them.

In 1759, Dr. Samuel Johnson wrote, "The trade of advertising is now so near to perfection that it is not easy to propose any improvement."[3] That was written in 1759, folks, probably with a quill pen. I don't want to make the same mistake in this book. So, I repeat. Learn the rules in this book. Then break them. Break them all. Find something new. I'm convinced it's out there.

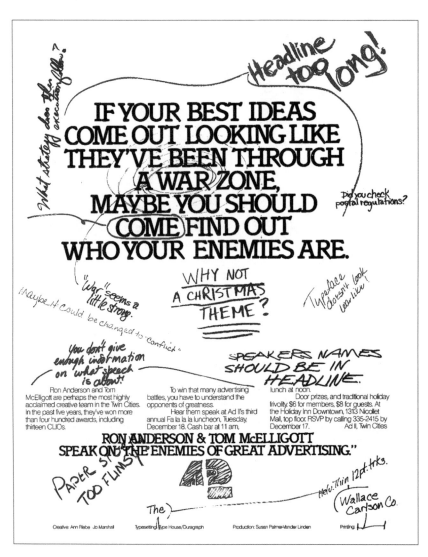

Figure 8.1 As it turns out, there are actually quite a few things "more powerful than an idea whose time has come." There's the marketing manager, the product manager, the research department, the CEO, the CFO, and that loud, opinionated guy who shows up at every focus group.

8

Only the Good Die Young

The enemies of advertising

IN A PERFECT WORLD, IT WORKS LIKE THIS. You come up with a great ad. You take it over to the client and they agree it solves the problem and approve it for production.

In my 18 years in the business, this has happened three times. What usually happens is your ad dies. I don't know why it is this way, but it is. Get ready for it. It doesn't matter how good your ad is, it can die.

I once watched a client kill a campaign between sips of coffee. Two months in the making and he killed it all—every TV spot, every magazine, and every newspaper ad—with one chirpy line.

"Good first effort."

The thing to remember is, clients are perfectly within their rights to do this. We are in a service business. And our service isn't over when we present something we like. It's over when we present something *they* like. The trick is to do both the first time.

There are good clients out there. Bless them. When you have one, serve them well. Work nights for them. Work weekends. You will produce the best work of your career on their behalf.

And then there's the other kind: the "hard" clients, the "challenging" clients, or, as we say when using English, the bad clients. Fortunately, good clients outnumber them. But the bad ones are out there and you need to be able to spot them. Here are some of the kinds I've run into in my career. Let me rephrase. Here are some of the kinds that have run over me in my career.

There isn't a lot you can do about them. They're like mines buried in the field of advertising. Try not to step on any.

THE SISYPHUS ACCOUNT

Those familiar with Greek mythology know Sisyphus, the king of Corinth. The gods sentenced him to an eternity in hell, pushing a large rock up a hill. He'd get it to the top, only to watch it roll to the bottom where his job awaited him again.

So how do you spot an account like Sisyphus Corp? By the smell of foam core—that stiff board that agencies use to mount ads for presentations. You'll notice the smell the minute you get off the agency elevator. They won't tell you what it is during the interview, but you'll find out soon enough.

The creative director comes in and says, "I'm putting you on Sisy-Corp. You're perfect for them." You'd be excited about it, were it not for the pallid look of the passing secretary who overhears your assignment.

Soon though, you start to catch on. One day you're walking down the hall and you notice you've never seen an ad for Sisyphus displayed up on the wall. Not one. Then you see the delivery guys from the local art supplies company; they're in the lobby again with another cart full of foam core. *(Weren't they just here yesterday?)* Then one day you're looking for markers in the storeroom and you find 200 dead storyboards for Sisyphus, all of them great ideas, all dead as doornails, and all hidden in the corner like Henry VIII's closet of heads.

In the interview they told you Sisyphus Corp was the next VW. The next Energizer Bunny. "We're turning it around." But now you're starting to understand: Corporations like Sisyphus don't want to actually *run* advertising. They want to look at it. They want to talk about it. They want to have meetings about it. But they won't run an ad. Not this year anyway.

"If we were to run advertising—we're not, but if we *were* to run an ad—could you show us what it might look like?"

You've just been handed a shovel and told to feed the Foam Core Furnace. You will work as hard as somebody whose ads are actually being published. You'll spend the same late nights and long weekends and order in the same pizza. But when the year is over, you'll have nothing to show for it but some ads mounted on foam core and a pizza gut.

This kind of account, while it can drive you crazy, isn't the worst. They're like blind giants, a Cyclops with something under his contact lens. They're big. They have money. And if they lumber about and head in the wrong direction it hardly matters. As long as they make their numbers, they don't care. They've lost the entrepreneurial spirit. Winning isn't important. Not losing is.

There isn't much you can do about this kind of account. There's an old saying: "The only way out is through." Sometimes it's best simply to feed the beast its daily minimum requirement of concepts and then sneak out to a movie when the foam core gods aren't hungry. Call it "paying your dues." After you've put in a few months papering the walls of your client's meeting rooms, appeal to your creative director. Show him your battle scars. He may put a fresh team in front of Sisyphus's rock.

Sisyphus isn't the worst kind of account. Not by a long shot. There's another enemy of good advertising. Fear.

THE MEAT PUPPET

A very talented woman named Lois Korey, an ad star from the '60s, described this kind of account:

> Clients seem to get the advertising they deserve. The good ones, they're risk takers. They're willing to risk failures for extraordinary success. . . . The bad clients? Fear dribbles down from the top. No one says so, in so many words, but you know no risks will be tolerated, no rules will be broken, that mediocrity is the measure by which your work will be weighed.[1]

Fear dribbles down from the top, says Korey. The Chinese have a more colorful phrase: "A fish stinks from the head."

You can actually smell it on the vice presidents, the fear. No amount of Roll-On's gonna cover up their terror of the boss. It may be their boss, or their boss's boss; it doesn't matter.

But the boss has done a terrible thing to these vice presidents. He has put them in charge of something they're not in charge of. The nameplate outside their cubicle may sport words like "Assistant Director of Marketing." But they are not directing marketing or anything else for that matter. They are, in effect, meat puppets.

Invisible strings, thin but powerful, dangle down from management and are attached to every part of their bodies. Everything these guys do, everything they think, every memo they write, every decision they don't put off, will be second-guessed.

When you're a meat puppet, what you do is say no. An ad lands on your desk, and that invisible string connected to your hand makes you reach for the big "NO" stamp, pulls it back over the ad, and wham!

"NO!"

I have seen fear completely unravel a meat puppet.

She was the director of marketing for a large corporation whose name you'd recognize. She needed a TV spot, just one 30-second spot, for a new product being introduced the following spring. It was a great product. It deserved a big, wonderful introductory spot. We worked hard and presented an idea we believed was very good.

We flew in. Shook hands. Found a room with an easel, did our setup, and unveiled. She looked at the storyboard, looked at her notebook, then wrote something down. (When clients do this, I always assume it's: "Begin new-agency search immediately.") She looked up and said, "I just don't like it."

The strategy wasn't the problem. How we were saying it wasn't the problem.

"I just don't like it."

Good clients are allowed this. If they're buying decent work most of the time, well, they deserve to have those simple human reservations we all feel now and then. We decide to let her play the "Just don't like it" card. Fine. We go back. Time is running out, so we bring three storyboards to the next meeting. Luckily we're on a streak and all three are good. We'd have been happy to go with any one.

"I just don't like it."

"All three?"

"I just don't like it."

"What is it you don't like?"

"I can't say." And then she said the one thing all the really bad clients say sooner or later. "I'll know it when I see it."

Copywriter and author Dick Wasserman said this phrase is tantamount to a general telling his armies, "March off in all directions, and when I see where one of you is headed, I'll have a better fix on where I'd like the rest of you to go."

And so we marched off in all directions. Meeting after meeting was adjourned with, "I just don't like it." The boards piled up. After awhile, we didn't bother to fly in for meetings and started faxing the boards, always getting the same answer.

Some 25 boards passed before her. And 25 died. I assure you, we didn't give up. It was a good product. A fallow field lay before us. We presented good work right up to the end.

"I just don't like it."

Time began to run out. Directors' January schedules were filling up. The media was bought and the client was panicking. Client panic sometimes works in the agency's favor. Not this time. She asked for more. In the final phone meeting, the agency simply refused to provide any more boards.

And the client unraveled. I mean, she completely fell apart.

I remember listening to her voice on the speakerphone, hearing it begin to waver. She began to cry and then, God help me, *beg* like a junkie for more work.

She had become addicted to indecision.

"Come on! It doesn't even have to be a 30. Gimme a stinkin' 15. I'll take a 15! You got to have some 15s! Oh baby, baby, come to momma with another board." (Okay, she didn't say exactly that, but . . . she said exactly that.) I'd never seen anything like it. It got worse, too.

Somehow, around board #29, she bought something. The agency wasn't proud of the piece. We were just holding our noses, hoping to simply produce the thing and be done with it. (This project had become what we call a "turd boomerang." One of those awful projects you throw out the window and it comes back in the door.) A second-tier director was chosen. A location in Miami was scouted and approved. There was a listless prepro meeting. Sets built. The team assembled in Florida the night before the cameras rolled. And the phone rang.

In the 11th hour, in the 59th minute, and in the tail end of the 59th second, the client's antiperspirant failed again. "I just don't like it."

The agency was forced to come up with a new concept and do it under the constraints of an existing set and a locked-off budget. Which is a lot like being told to build a plane and here's a coffee can, a crayon, and an old copy of *Sports Illustrated.* It was insane. It was like that famous line from journalist Bill Mellor: "We are sorry. But the editor's indecision is final."

These incredible dervishlike turnarounds are known as "doing a 360°." It's like doing a 180°, but twice. It could be argued this client did a 540° or even a 720°. (A 900° was once observed in Brussels, but no verification was available as this book went to press.)

The agency had to go back to the drawing board yet again. This time, getting the idea took just ten minutes. The tired writer and the dispirited art director walked to the end of a nearby pier and lit cigarettes.

Idea #30 limped into the writer's mind like a sick dog with its ribs showing, and the writer said, "Okay, what if we did this?"

The art director looked at the dog. The dog looked up at the art director.

"Fine."

They took their sick little animal of an idea and walked it back down the dock toward the nearest phone.

The client loved it.

It should come as no surprise that the final spot sucked. It was so bad we were trying to change channels on it during the final editing session. "See what else is on," someone would say. What *is* surprising is how the client later decided they didn't like it and blamed the agency. "Why aren't our commercials as good as the work you do for your other clients?"

The spot never aired. I swear this happened.

There is a list I've seen posted on bulletin boards in many agencies. One of those jokes that get xeroxed and passed around, then faxed and xeroxed again until the type decays. This was the list:

"THE SIX PHASES OF AN ADVERTISING PROJECT"

1. Enthusiasm
2. Disillusionment

3. Panic

4. Search for the guilty

5. Punishment of the innocent

6. Praise and honors for the nonparticipants

What was once a joke tacked to a bulletin board had become grim reality. What began with enthusiasm ended as a new-agency search.

Funny thing though. While the account did leave the agency, a month later we heard the woman was fired.

And, wouldn't you know it, in her absence the client's advertising improved. Which is always a little hard to take. I mean, the mature thing to do is wash the blood off your hands, wave good-bye to an account, and wish them the best. But you secretly wish your old girl-friend, after she dumps you, ends up dealing crack from a culvert or pushing a mop at the Bun 'n Burger.

I had another client who was a meat puppet, working in a company run by fear. He was about as far down the corporate food chain as you could get—cubicle plankton. He even looked the part: that pale-white kind of guy who always gets killed in the first five minutes of a movie. Yet, to get an ad approved, you had to run it by this guy. And a bullet from his ratty little Saturday night special was as deadly as any other.

He was perhaps the tensest person I ever met. One morning, he was seen standing in front of the company coffee machine holding an empty cup, growling through clenched teeth, "Brew, goddammit." He had such high blood pressure, we worried that if he sustained even a paper cut, arterial spray would redden the ceiling.

But, as scared as he was, he had a little power game he ran. It was brilliant. Whenever you presented ads to him for his approval, he wouldn't look at you. Or the ads. Wouldn't look at all. He'd just stare down at his legal pad in front of him.

There you were, having taken a two-hour plane ride, lugging your portfolio in and out of cabs to arrive in his conference room. You did your setup and then presented the ads, ta-da! . . . to the top of his head. And if it was a visual concept, it drove you crazy. Because you found yourself having to use words to explain an image that you came up with to avoid using words in the first place.

He, too, was a meat puppet. Unable to make any decision without imagined repercussions from above, he chose to make none and instead passed his decision onto the next guy up the food chain.

There is nothing you can do about a meat puppet. Your boss is going to have to go above him, to whomever's yanking his strings. Such a decision is not yours to make and you'll need one of your higher-ups to talk with one of theirs. Sometimes it works. You may discover the client culture isn't in fact fear-based and that your contact person is living in a backwater of fear he created on his own.

PABLUM PARK

It's a ten o'clock meeting on Monday morning at Martini, Yesman & Longlunch. Coats come off and hands are shaken. Coffee poured and ties flattened. Everybody's excited because the client, the big regional power company, wants a new campaign.

"Okay," asks the agency, "about what?"

"Well, just about us. You know. *Us.*"

"Okay, but what about . . . *us?*"

"We care."

"You care?"

"We care."

"You care about what?"

"We just . . . *care.*"

"Okay, I get the caring. I get it. But what is it you care *about?*"

"Why do we have to care about anything in particular? Just a general sort of caring I think would be fine. In fact, Dick here was just saying on the way to the agency how that would be a workable theme-slogan sort of thing—'We Care.' "

Dick nods, sagely.

Uh-oh. It's a client with absolutely nothing to say. You are now entering Pablum Park. Abandon all relevance ye who enter here.

A power company is a good example of this kind of client. There's nothing they *can* say without ticking customers off. Why they advertise at all is beyond me. Where else are you going to "shop" for electricity? (*"Oh, I think I'll use that plug over there."*) Many hospitals and health care plans have the same problem. They can't say "Our doctors are better than their doctors." They can't say "We cost less." They can, however, say, "We *care.*"

So the Pablum Machine is turned on and everything begins to run together in a saccharine slurry of Caring and Sharing and People Helping People. In fact, Pablum Park is populated entirely by "People People®."

"We're not just a giant corporation. We're People People® Helping People."

In Pablum Park, the police are "People Protecting People from People." Morticians are "Living People Helping Dead People." And lawyers are "People, Trying to *Be* People, Trying People."

If you watch even a half hour of television, you'll see many commercials spouting drivel. Peel away the bluster and bombast, the jingles and clichés, and you'll find drivel. Nothing of substance. Words that sort of *sound* like you should be paying attention to them, but are ultimately empty.

The best drivel I've ever read was in a wonderful parody called *Patriotic Spot—60 Seconds* by Ellis Weiner. I reprint it here in abbreviated form.

> You're waking up, America. It's morning—and you're waking up to live life like you've never lived it before. Say hello to a whole new way of being awake, America. Say hello to us. . . .
>
> We're watching you, America. We're watching you when you work—because, America, you work hard. And we know that afterward you've got a mighty big thirst. Not just a thirst for the best beer you can find. But a thirst for living. A thirst for years of experience. America, you're thirsty. . . .
>
> America, say hello to something new. Say hello to quality. Quality you can see. Quality you can feel. Quality you can say hello to. (How do you spell "quality," America? *Real* quality—quality you can trust? The same way we've been spelling it for over a hundred and fifty years.) . . .
>
> We're Number One. You're Number One. You're a winner, America. And we know what you're thinking. We know how you feel. How do we know? Because we take the time to tell you. We take the time to care.
>
> And it pays off. We're here, America. And the next time you're here—the next time we can tell you who we are and what we do—we'll be doing what we do best.[2]

You're not completely without hope with this kind of client. But it'll take some work on your part. Every client has a story. Even the big, ugly ones with names like "Syntheti-Corp" have a story that can be made relevant and meaningful to the average reader.

International Paper's campaign by Ogilvy & Mather back in the '80s is a good example. International was a faceless corporation that made a product not famous for brand loyalty—paper.

Yet their campaign of award-winning ads was exquisitely read-

How to write with style

By Kurt Vonnegut

International Paper asked Kurt Vonnegut, author of such novels as "Slaughterhouse-Five," "Jailbird" and "Cat's Cradle," to tell you how to put your style and personality into everything you write.

Newspaper reporters and technical writers are trained to reveal almost nothing about themselves in their writings. This makes them freaks in the world of writers, since almost all of the other ink-stained wretches in that world reveal a lot about themselves to readers. We call these revelations, accidental and intentional, elements of style.

These revelations tell us as readers what sort of person it is with whom we are spending time. Does the writer sound ignorant or informed, stupid or bright, crooked or honest, humorless or playful – ? And on and on.

Why should you examine your writing style with the idea of improving it? Do so as a mark of respect for your readers, whatever you're writing. If you scribble your thoughts any which way, your readers will surely feel that you care nothing about them. They will mark you down as an egomaniac or a chowderhead – or, worse, they will stop reading you.

The most damning revelation you can make about yourself is that you do not know what is interesting and what is not. Don't you yourself like or dislike writers

mainly for what they choose to show you or make you think about? Did you ever admire an empty-headed writer for his or her mastery of the language? No.

So your own winning style must begin with ideas in your head.

1. Find a subject you care about

Find a subject you care about and which you in your heart feel others should care about. It is this genuine caring, and not your games with language, which will be the most compelling and seductive element in your style.

I am not urging you to write a novel, by the way – although I would not be sorry if you wrote one, provided you genuinely cared about something. A petition to the mayor about a pothole in front of your house or a love letter to the girl next door will do.

2. Do not ramble, though

I won't ramble on about that.

3. Keep it simple

As for your use of language: Remember that two great masters of language, William Shakespeare and James Joyce, wrote sentences which were almost childlike when their subjects were most profound. "To be or not to be?" asks Shakespeare's Hamlet. The longest word is three letters long. Joyce, when he was frisky, could put together a sentence as intricate and as glittering as a necklace for Cleopatra, but my favorite sentence in his short story "Eveline" is this one: "She was tired." At that point in the story, no other words could break the heart of a reader as those three words do.

Simplicity of language is not only reputable, but perhaps even sacred. The *Bible* opens with a sentence well within the writing skills of a lively fourteen-year-old. "In the beginning God created the heaven and the earth."

4. Have the guts to cut

It may be that you, too, are capable of making necklaces for Cleopatra, so to speak. But your eloquence should be the servant of the ideas in your head. Your rule might be this: If a sentence, no matter how excellent, does not illuminate your subject in some new and useful way, scratch it out.

5. Sound like yourself

The writing style which is most natural for you is bound to echo the speech you heard when a child. English was the novelist Joseph Conrad's third language, and much that seems piquant in his use of English was no doubt colored by his first language, which was Polish. And lucky indeed is the writer who has grown up in Ireland, for the English spoken there is so amusing and musical. I myself grew up in Indianapolis, where common speech sounds like a band saw cutting galvanized tin,

Should I act upon the urgings that I feel, or remain passive and thus cease to exist?

To be or not to be?

"Keep it simple. Shakespeare did, with Hamlet's famous soliloquy."

Figure 8.2   Long-copy ads can be great. Even if a customer doesn't read every word, it looks like the company has a lot to say.

able (Fig. 8.2). Above a spread filled with long, well-written copy were headlines like: "How to improve your vocabulary." Or "How to enjoy poetry." Each ad was authored by a marquee-name like James Dickey or Kurt Vonnegut. And at the end of the ads, the copy seamlessly brought you around to International's take on the deal: "We believe in the power of the printed word."

Figure 8.2 (Continued)

———

THE KONCEPT KRUSHER 2000®

This actually happened.

After several weeks of work, we finished a campaign for a large account and presented it to the client. They approved it, "pending research."

The account guys sent the boards to an advertising research firm retained by the client. A week later, the results came back. We'd scored okay with the traditional focus group tests. But we'd failed the "Andrea" test and had to start all over.

"What is the 'Andrea' test?" I asked the client.

With a straight face, she said, "Well, the thing is, we give your storyboards to a guy there at the research place. And he and another guy, they take it into a room and they close the door and then come out about, oh, three hours later with the results. And we know if your spot works. Yours didn't. I'm sorry."

"But what did they *do* in there?"

"The research firm tells us that's proprietary."

"Pro. . . . can I *talk* to this 'Andrea'?"

" 'Andrea' is just the name for the test. There *is* no Andrea and the methodology is proprietary, as I've said. They don't have to tell us what they do in there. The results they come out with always seem to be right on the money."

I stood there, blinking. The client, I'm sure, thought I was trying to think of some counterargument. But what I was thinking about was social work. (*"I like people. I could help someone, maybe a little kid. It would be nice to get away. Peru or something. Maybe a little shack. Wouldn't be so bad."*)

I came to in the cab on the way to the airport, holding a fat spiral notebook full of all the things wrong with my ads, courtesy of "Andrea."

Clients who rely on test results to approve work will always be with us. There's no escaping it. That's the good news. The bad news is, with some clients, research will kill all of your work *all* the time.

Many large corporations have whole floors devoted to advertising-slash-research and they have it down to a system. They feed your storyboards into one end of a process that's very much like a machine, with a name like, I don't know, "Koncept-Krusher 2000."

As your campaign goes through the device, you hear all kinds of nasty things happening . . . (*"It's negative!" Muffled sounds. "We can't say that." Unidentified thwacking noise. "Why can't they all be happy?"*) . . . and what comes out the other end you wouldn't want to air on a clothesline, much less network television.

The *really* bad news is that there isn't a thing you can do about it. Once these huge research machines are in place, they're usually there to stay. And no good idea will *ever* get out alive. Generally, it's the older, larger clients who've been advertising for years that have an overheated K/K 2000 down in the basement, running day and night.

I worked for several clients like this, where I think I did some of the best work of my career. But you've never seen it. On one particularly baneful project I remember, the Krusher must've been set on "high" because it went through hundreds, literally hundreds, of storyboards.

After I burned out on the project, the agency threw other people at the snapping jaws of the research machine. And then another team. And another. A full year later, the Krusher spit out this tepid little storyboard that both research and the client had approved.

There on the conveyer belt lay the TV spot—a trembling, pathetic thing that did not like being looked at directly. A sort of marketing Frankenstein—chunks of different departmental agendas and mandates, all sewn together by focus groups and researchers into something that looked like a TV spot but was in fact an abomination. We should have hammered a spike through its heart right there.

THE BULLY

There is another kind of bad account. The account run by the Bully client. Bullies anywhere are bad. But Bullies with power are enough, as Anne Lamott says, to make Jesus drink himself to sleep.

Some bullies may be born that way, but most develop over many years, like wine gone sour in a forgotten cellar. They come out of the cellar with a vast amount of knowledge, all of it wrong down to the syllable. The one I'm thinking of had been in the business some 20 years when I was put on his account.

He had spent most of his career on a second-rate brand of beer and was personally responsible for one of the worst campaigns ever to foul a TV set. And he was so *proud* of that beer campaign. Women with big breasts. Wild beach parties with lots of what he'd call "jiggle." And always ending with that tired old shot, a bartender holding two frosty bottles in each hand, offering them to the camera. "Product ID!" he'd say.

He would brag about this awful campaign, using it as a ruler: measuring our work by it one day, smacking our hands with it the next. When it was "just us guys" in the room, he'd say, "You wanna know why that campaign worked? I'll tellya why that campaign worked. We had girls with them big ol' titties and trucks and everything."

I'm not kidding. He said that. It was like every nightmare Gloria Steinem ever had about the way some men behave behind closed corporate doors. He was a pig.

Even his boss knew his beer campaign stank and would occasionally interrupt him in mid-brag to tell him so. The Bully would good-naturedly chuck him on the shoulder and remind him of the slight upward drift of his beer's sales curve.

He projected his own inadequacies onto the market and made the mistake of thinking that the customer is none too bright. And it was reflected in the advertising he forced all of his agencies to do. Pile-driving, no-nonsense nonsense.

During your career in advertising, you will meet this man. He will know nothing about advertising but will wield great power. "All hat and no cattle," I've heard him described. No argument will be eloquent enough to sway him from his sledgehammer approach to advertising. There is no poetry in the man. No subtlety. He is a paper tiger. A tin-pot despot lording over his little product fiefdom, spouting rules from advertising's Bronze Age, and pointing to modest sales increases whenever his excesses and crudities are exposed.

And the day all intelligence in advertising dies, he should be brought in for questioning.

HALLWAY BEAST #1: THE HACK

Yes, clients can misbehave. Thank God, most of them don't. And to account for all that awful work you see on TV every night, those bad clients must have a few friends on the agency side. They do.

Like everything else in life, America's list of agencies makes up a big bell curve. There are a few truly great agencies, then a whole bunch of agencies that are just okay, and then a few shriekingly bad ones.

To get off to the right start in this business, you're going to need to know how to spot those bad agencies. And it's not as easy as you think. Just because an agency has a few commercials in the latest awards annual doesn't mean you want to work there.

What you've got to do is, during your interviews, look for the Hack.

The first warning sign that you're in the presence of a Hack is that he'll somehow bring up his One Good Ad from Way Back. He won't call it that. In fact, he'll show it to you and say something like, "This is the kind of work we do here." That's when you notice the ad is on brittle, yellowing paper from a magazine like *Collier's*.

All Hacks have one of these ads. They made their name on it. They've been riding its tired, old back for decades and look about as silly doing it as Adam West now looks in his old Batman suit.

It can be a great ad. Doesn't matter. Ask yourself, what else have they done? Talented people with a gift for advertising keep doing great work, time and again, for a variety of clients.

Another warning sign that should send your Hack-O-Meter into the red is how they talk. And how they do talk. In fact, talk is all a Hack can do, being incapable as he is of producing an ad that a fly won't lay eggs on. He'll know the buzzwords. And worse, he'll have a few of his own. "At this agency, we believe in advertising with Clutter-Busting® Power." If you hear something like this, just drop your portfolio and run. You can put together another book. Just run. Don't risk the elevator. Go for the stairs.

Agencies are the way they are for a reason. It's no accident they're doing awful work. They have clients on one side asking for awful work, Hacks on the other side giving it to them, and a guy in the middle counting all the money. Talk is cheap. Especially talk about how "we're going to turn this place around." If you hear this phrase, *you* should turn around. Again, go for the stairs.

The quintessential giveaway, however, is the creative director who denigrates creativity in general and awards shows in particular. This was the kid in the playground who didn't have a big red ball and so he told the other kids, "Big red balls are *stupid.*" He can't do it. So, of course, he's going to denigrate it.

Some of these guys kill ideas simply because they're unable to generate ideas of their own. In fact, to kill what you've come up with actually seems like an idea to them. They'll go: "Hey wait! Shhhhh! . . . I have an idea! Let's *not* do your idea!" Their ideas are like antimatter. They don't really exist until yours does and when they meet, they're both gone in an instant.

In an interview, this guy will look you straight in the eye and say, "Creativity is overrated. Client sales is what we're all about." He'll get out a case history. Show you some commercials he'll call "hardworking" and then tap his finger on a number at the bottom of the results page. "This, my little friend, is what we do."

Someday I'd like to try an experiment. It will cost $40 million. I'll give a fifth-grader a brand name and tell him to shoot a commercial. Whatever he comes up with, I'll spend the rest of the $39-some million airing on prime time. In a couple of months, I'll bet Little Jimmy can take off his baseball glove and tap his finger on a similar sales increase. The point is, with a two-ton sledgehammer even a fifth-grader can ring the bell at the top. (I suspect Mr. Whipple's war chest of several trillion had something to do with his high recall scores.)

In 1981, Fallon McElligott Rice opened its doors, running a house ad with the headline:

> A new advertising agency for companies that would rather outsmart the competition than outspend them.

And that's exactly what they did. They created inexpensive, highly creative commercials that outshone and outperformed many of Madison Avenue's high-dollar clients.

My old boss, Pat Fallon, said,* "Some of us call the right execution 'creative leverage.' It carries the message effectively and is a cost-effective tool when budget does not allow omnipresent 'media leverage.' Disciplined creativity is often, as Ed McCabe said years ago, the last remaining legal means you have to gain an unfair advantage over the competition."[3]

---

*Reprinted with permission from the August 7, 1989, issue of *Advertising Age.* Copyright, Crain Communications Inc. 1989.

Compare that quotation from the chairman of Fallon McElligott with this quotation from Chairman Hack. I can't print this man's name, but to a national trade magazine he said blithely and without shame, "Sheer repetition can build awareness and equity for a client even if an ad is not considered creatively brilliant. A dumb dollar beats a smart dime any day."

"Sheer repetition?" If I were this guy's client, I'd take my dumb dollar over to an agency that can give me ten times the wallop with a dime's worth of sheer brilliance.

Hacks get easier to spot as they feed and prosper. In their mature years, they sprout long titles, some growing up to ten inches in length. Recently, I saw a picture of a Hack in an industry magazine, and below it, this title: "Senior Vice-President/Vice Chairman/Chief Creative Officer North America/Worldwide Manager/Global Coordinator." I'm not kidding—word for word.

Agencies may keep them on, sort of as expensive hood ornaments. They'll trot them out at big pitches, but during the rest of the year they'll give them what I call a "Nerf account"—something they can bat around without hurting themselves or anyone else. They are well known, as one wag put it, chiefly for being well known.

A closing thought on Hacks. One of the great things about this business is that you'll be surrounded by vibrant, interesting, and genuinely nice people. I don't know why the industry attracts them, it just does.

And Hacks are no exception. Most of the ones I've known are just as nice a person as you could want to meet. After office hours, they're great fishing buddies, loving mothers, and intelligent bridge partners.

But I warn you against joining their team during working hours. As a junior, you'll learn bad habits from them, habits that will be hard to break, even when you come under the tutelage of more talented teachers. We improve by surrounding ourselves with people whose work we admire.

THE GOLDEN HANDCUFFS

If you take a job at a big, dull agency, you may, without your seeing it happen, slip into a pair of "golden handcuffs." That big agency may be willing to pay you a lot of money to crank out the dull ads. You get used to the money. A couple of years go by and as your bank account fills with money, your book fills with bad ads—ads you can't show without embarrassment or explanation.

Agencies will do all kinds of silly things to keep you happy at your desk cranking out bad stuff. I remember at one agency they started handing out vice presidencies like candy from a Pez dispenser. Anybody who complained or was seen putting his portfolio together was suddenly a vice president.

After awhile though, it seemed almost everybody in the creative department was a VP, and the distinction began to lose its luster. That didn't stop them. They just started handing out "*secret*" vice presidencies.

The boss would motion you into his office. He'd say, "We love your work. You're gonna be a superstar. So we're making you a *vice president,* but . . . uh, we don't want you to tell anyone. Some people, well, they aren't as good as you and aren't being promoted."

By the time I left, the entire creative department was full of "superstars" who were vice presidents, half on the up-and-up, and half "secret" vice presidents. The agency where I work now is full of incredibly talented people. But there's not one vice president. The agency places no value on titles, only talent.

Most of the time, these "assistant vice presidencies" and other titles don't add up to much anyway. I had a friend who worked for a large, stuffy old agency. The morning after he was promoted, he was standing outside his cubicle chatting with a coworker. The kid from the mail room shows up with a hammer and says, "Your name Buchner?" My friend nods yes. The kid proceeds to wedge one corner of the cubicle open, hammers in a modular two-foot extension piece, says "Congratulations" and walks away.

HALLWAY BEAST #2: THE PRIMA DONNA

The Prima Donna is the writer or art director who thinks he is God's gift to advertising.

I've known a couple of PDs in my day, and for this section I swirl together my memories of the few I've known to paint a picture of one very bitter, talented person.

He had that one dead giveaway, something all PDs share—the Swagger. That *walk* people get when they think their DNA is better than everybody else's. Oops, there he goes now, down the hallway. And in his hand, a paper bearing his latest brilliant headline.

Why they develop a Swagger, I don't know. I mean, if that paper was a blueprint for world peace instead of a coupon ad for Jell-O, okay, sashay a little bit. But the PD seems to have forgotten what he does for a living. He's a word-slinging schmuck like the rest of us. But you'll never convince a Prima Donna he's the same species as we.

Wherever the Prima Donna is swaggering, when he gets there you can bet he'll have something nasty to say about either how excruciatingly dumb account executives are or what blind bastards his little sty-full of client-pigs are.

But *you,* you're okay—that is, if the Prima Donna is standing within ten feet of you. PDs obey what I call the "10-Foot Pinhead Rule." Anyone farther than ten feet from the Prima Donna is a pinhead. He'll walk into your office and say, "Oh, you wouldn't *believe* the pinhead I was just talking to." Of course, the rule applies when he leaves your office. Eleven feet down the hallway, he'll be telling whoever he's with, "God, I'm glad we left *that* pinhead's office."

Prima Donnas would have made great Nazis, because they cultivate an air of entitlement and genetic superiority. Each one believes he is the center gear in capitalism's great machine. What the pen of Herr Donna writes today will tomorrow be on the lips of all the haggard supermarket moms he makes fun of in his off-hours.

You see, Prima Donnas have so *much* to teach us. If we would only listen. But as the years go by and he casts more of his pearls before swine, his poison ferments and his talons curl. Prima Donnas just get mean.

It's like this: When I look out of my tall office building, I think all the people look like ants. He thinks that when he's on the street.

There was this one Prima Donna I remember. His first day at work he called the office manager in and calmly directed that his desk be raised three inches. Three inches, I'm not kidding. Apparently, his keyboard had to be a certain distance from his chin to invoke his visions. When he could bully the producers into it, he would fly only first class. And any suggestions from coworkers on how to improve an ad were laughed off or explained away.

It got so bad finally that no art director would work with him. He was about to be fired, when he quit and took a job somewhere else.

The hurt and anger he left behind in the agency lingered for some time. Secretaries came out of hiding and admitted to farting in his office when he was gone. After awhile, we tried to be philosophical about his character. The best we could say about him was: "If you cut him open, you'd find a heart of gold. And if you didn't, hey, you've cut him open."

HALLWAY BEAST #3: THE WHINER

Lord knows, I've been one of these. And in my early years, I wasted a lot of time doing it. (Does this chapter count as whining? Don't answer.)

It has been said that whining is simply anger coming through a very small hole. If so, then the Whiner is a very angry little man.

What he whines about most is his job. And he whines *all* the time. All of his clients suck. All account executives suck. All planning sucks. The sad part is if he could just convert half the energy he spends whining in the hallways to working in his office, he'd be doing better work. Yes, that work might die because sometimes a client does, in fact, suck. But that's the breaks of the business. Get over it.

When the Whiner moves on to that agency he says is so much better, it's the old truism: "Wherever you go in life, there you are." To his horror, he discovers ad agencies are pretty much the same all over. There are hard clients, misguided research, and unreasonable deadlines everywhere, and because that's all he focuses on, these Harpies will follow him throughout all of his sad days.

I'm not saying you can't whine. It's good to let off some steam now and then. True Whining, however, has a vituperative edge to it. It's toxic. Pestilential. There's no hope in it. After awhile, you wonder why Whiners don't just leave the business altogether.

Cut to the next scene, the Whiner's new job at the shoe store: "I should get a job over at Foot Locker. Those guys are so good. This place sucks."

HALLWAY BEAST #4: THE HOUR GOBBLER

This beast isn't a person. It's a thing. The Meeting. If you see one, run.

Run, little pony, run and *never* look back.

If the wheels of capitalism ever grind to a halt, the agenda of a meeting will be found caught in the gears. And in the advertising business, meetings thrive like mutant weeds, making actual work impossible.

There are meetings with doughnuts and meetings without doughnuts. Meetings to talk about ads you're going to do and meetings to talk about the ads you just did. All these meetings will be held in small, windowless rooms heated to forehead-dampening temperatures by slide-projector bulbs and all held during that torpid postlunch lull around 2:30.

As a junior, you probably should just shrug and show up for any meeting you get "memo'd" on. But as your radar develops, you'll start to be able to detect which meetings are important—where plans are made and things get done—and which aren't.

The ones I'm talking about are those meetings that are called because somebody needed something to do. "Background" meetings. Or "touching base" meetings. These aren't called because decisions need to be made. They're just called. And oh how they go on. I was in one of these Hour Gobblers once and I swear time actually stopped. I'm not kidding. Swear to God, as plain as day, the second hand on the wall clock just *stopped*. No more ticktock. Just . . . tick . . . and that was it.

It was a particularly useless meeting three hours long. Just when we thought we were going to get out, someone raised his hand and asked a question—the kind of tired, lifeless query I call a "meeting extender." A meeting extender is a question like: "Well, Bill, how do those figures compare with the results from *Chicago?*" That's when the clock stopped and began to sag like a Dali painting.

Speakerphone meetings are the worst. And the worst of the worst is the three-way speakerphone, client-on-a-car-phone conference call meeting. There you are, eight nervous people all huddled around a little black box, listening to an art director in LA describe a picture nobody can see to a client nobody can hear.

Ending a meeting is an art it pays to develop. When the business at hand seems at an end even though the meeting is not, start stacking your papers together, evening up the edges, the way news anchors do at the end of their broadcasts. It's body language that says, "Well, nothing interesting is going to happen anymore in *this* room."

I hate it when I get sucked into an Hour Gobbler and have no work I can sneak into the meeting. I usually start writing jokes to myself to pass the time. In one meeting, I remember trying to make my buddy Bob Barrie laugh and instead blew my own cover. I started writing a joke: "Bob's List of Things to Do." I thought I'd just slip it under his nose. Try to crack him up. So I started scribbling:

BOB'S LIST OF THINGS TO DO:

1. Ointment on rash??
2. Rotate bricks under car in front yard.
3. Apologize to that kid's parents.
4. Wash blood out of clown suit.
5. Peek under scab.

When I wrote "Peek under scab," I did one of those bursting-laugh-out-loud kind of explosions and the whole room stopped thinking about Chicago and glared at me for an explanation. I simply had to fess up: "Hey, I'm sorry, I just thought of something funny, completely unrelated to these proceedings. I'm very sorry. Please continue."

But the image of Bob Barrie peeking under a knee scab finally did me in. I just collapsed, boneless, and had to excuse myself from the room.

But it got me out of the meeting.

Yet as much as I try to avoid meetings, all the really important stuff in this business ultimately happens in one meeting—the client presentation.

This is where all the hard work you've done lives or dies. And where the future audience of a storyboard is decided. Will it be 500 million people seeing your TV commercial on the Super Bowl? Or a janitor who glances at the big board with funny drawings before cramming it into the rolling garbage can?

It's an important meeting. Be prepared.

Figure 9.1   In focus groups, bad things happen to your storyboards. Very bad things.

9

Pecked to Death by Ducks

Presenting and protecting your work

ABOUT 20 PERCENT OF YOUR TIME in the advertising business will be spent thinking up ads; 80 percent will be spent protecting them; and 30 percent doing them over.

A screenwriter was looking out on the parking lot at Universal Studios one day. It occurred to him, said this article, that every one of those cars was parked there by somebody who came to stop him from doing his movie.

The similarity to advertising is chilling. The elevator cables in your client's building will fairly groan hauling up all the people intent on killing your best stuff.

When word gets around the client offices that the agency's here to present ideas, vice presidents and assistant vice presidents will appear out of the walls and storm the conference room like zombies in *Night of the Living Dead,* pounding on the door, hungry arms reaching in for the layouts, chanting, "Must kill. Must kill."

I have been in meetings where, after the last ad was presented, an eager young hatchet man raised his hand and asked his boss, "Can I be the first to say why I don't like it?"

I have been in meetings surrounded by so many vice presidents, I actually heard Custer whisper to me from the grave, "Man, I thought I had it bad. You guys are, like, *so* dead."

You will see ads killed in ways you didn't know things could be killed. You will see them eviscerated by blowhards bearing charts. You will see them garroted by quiet little men bearing political agendas. A comment from a passing janitor will pick off ads like cans from a fence post, and casual remarks by the chairman's wife will mow down whole campaigns like the first charge at Gallipoli.

Then there's the friendly fire to worry about. A stray memo from your agency's research department can send your campaign up in flaming foam core. Your campaign can also be "fragged" by the hallway remark of an angry coworker.

War widows received their telegrams from ashen-faced military chaplains. You, however, will look up from your desk to see an account executive, smiling.

"The client has some issues and concerns about your ads."

This is how account executives announce the death of your labors: "issues and concerns."

To understand the portent of this phrase, picture the men lying on the floor of that Chicago garage on St. Valentine's Day. Al Capone had issues and concerns with these men.

I've had account executives beat around the bush for 15 minutes before they could tell me the bad news. "Well, we had a good *meeting.*"

"Yes," you say, "but are the ads dead?"

"We learned a *lot.*"

"But are they dead?"

"Wellll, . . . they're not really dead. They're just in a new and better place."

When you next see your ads, they will be lying in state in the account executive's office. Maybe on the desk. Maybe down in between the desk and the wall. (So thoughtless.) Maybe they'll bear crease wounds where they were crudely folded during the pitch team's hasty medevac under fire.

But you'll remember them the way they were. *("They look so . . . so natural.")* Say your good-byes. Try to think about the good times. Then walk away and start preparing for the next attack. I hear the drums.

What follows are some arguments, perhaps quixotic, that may help protect your loved ones in future battles. If you find any of them useful, I recommend you commit them to memory. Go into meetings armed and with the safety off. It's my experience that what a client decides in a meeting stays decided.

PRESENTING YOUR WORK

Learn the client's corporate culture.

Spend as much time with the client as you can. Talk to the quiet guy from R&D. Tell jokes with the product managers. The more they know you, the more they're going to trust you. The more they trust you, the more likely they are to buy your strange and disgusting ideas.

But you're going to learn something about them, too. You're going to get a feel for the tone of this company. How far they will go. What they think is funny. You'll save yourself a lot of grief once you understand this. Remember, they see you as their brand ambassador. They're trusting you to accurately translate their corporate culture to the customer.

This doesn't mean doing the safe thing. It means if your client is a church, you probably shouldn't open your TV spot with that scene from *The Exorcist* where Linda Blair blow-chucks split pea soup on the priest.

Present your own work.

Nobody knows it better than you. Nobody has more invested in it than you. And if you screw up, you have nobody to blame but you.

Two addendums: (1) If you are a truly awful presenter, don't. At least not the big campaigns. Better to have a skilled account person or creative director sell them. (2) Learn to present. It's a skill, and like any other skill, the more you do it the better you'll get. Start small. Sell a small-space newspaper campaign. Present to the AEs. Just do it. Not being able to present your own work will handicap you throughout your entire career. Pilots can't be afraid of heights. It just doesn't work.

Practice selling your campaign before you go in to present.

Don't just wing it. I used to think winging it was cool. But that was just bravado. As if my ideas were so good they didn't need no stinking presentation. Wrong. Practice it.

Don't memorize a speech for your presentation.

Trying to memorize written material will make you nervous. You'll worry you're going to forget something. Write out a speech if it helps you organize your thoughts, but toss it when you're done. All you need to do is establish what marks you have to hit along the way and then make sure you hit them. "I need to make points A, B, and C." Once you see the light go on in a client's eyes regarding A, move on to B.

Don't be slick. Clients hate slick.

You know all those unfair stereotyped images we sometimes have about clients? Uptight, overly rational, number-crunching politicians. They've got a similar set of incorrect images about us. Slick, unctuous, glad-handing, promise-them-anything sycophants. Is it fair? No. But that's the thing about stereotypes. You're a little behind before you even start. So don't be slick.

But if you're not slick, what should you be?

Be yourself. Be smart. Be crisp, be to the point, be agreeable. Don't be something you aren't. It never works. You will appear disingenuous and so will your ideas.

Keep your "pre-ramble" to an absolute minimum. Start fast.

That doesn't mean start cold. It's likely you'll have to do some amount of setup. But make it crisp, to the point, and fast.

There is a wonderful book on the art of good presentations called *I Can See You Naked* by Ron Hoff. I recommend it. One of his points is this: The first 90 seconds of any presentation are crucial. "*Plunge* into your subject," writes Hoff. "Let there be no doubt that the subject has been engaged."[1]

In those first 90 seconds, the client is unconsciously sizing you up, making initial impressions, and probably deciding prematurely whether or not they're going to like what you have to say. As Hoff notes, "How many times have you heard someone in an audience [later] say, 'I knew . . . the minute she started, the very *first* minute, I just knew it was going to be sensational.'"[2]

So don't wade into the water. Dive.

Don't hand out materials before you present.

Stay in command of the room. The minute you hand a script to a client, you're competing with the script. Clients are human and naturally want to get to the good stuff. They'll start taking peeks.

In fact, when I present a TV storyboard, I'll sometimes cover up a number of frames to keep the client from getting ahead of me. Perhaps the best method is not to use a storyboard at all. A client usually looks at a storyboard and sees nine frames of "kooky, wacky stuff" and one frame of his logo. The math that goes through his head isn't pretty. It's usually better to work from a script and one key frame. Talk them through the broad strokes. Play a movie in their heads. And bring out a board later on only to discuss details.

Whatever you do, stay in control of the room's attention.

Maintain eye contact.

This may sound like a page out of Willy Loman's textbook, *So You Want to Be a Salesman.* But there's truth to it. If you're not looking the client square in the eyes every now and then, and making a human connection, why not just phone it in?

Don't go and get self-conscious about this and clumsily adopt some canned technique. "Okay, I'll make one eye contact every 30 seconds." Just stay aware of your client. Remember, you're not presenting so much as you're talking with somebody. Don't stay glued to the advertising you've got up on the wall. It's just a visual aid. You are the presentation. Turn around at key points in the action, says Hoff, and *punctuate* with your eyes.

Don't present your campaign as "risk-taking work." Clients hate that.

In the agency hallways, it's fine to talk about work being risk-taking. But it's just about the worst thing you can say to a product manager.

They don't want risk. They want certainty. Whether certainty is possible in this business remains in doubt, but clients definitely do *not* need to hear the R word.

Find other ways to describe your campaign. For instance, "It goes against the grain." Anything other than "risky" is more palatable to a client with his job on the line, a mortgage to pay, and two kids to put through reform school.

Okay, before we go further, I just want to say the next paragraph is *really* good. I worked a long time on it and I think you're really going to love it. In fact, it may be the best paragraph in this whole book.

Before you unveil your stuff, don't assure the client that "You are going to love this."

This is known as leading with your chin. Somebody's gonna take a swipe at it just to keep you humble.

As they say in law school, don't ask a question unless you already know the answer.

Same thing in presentations. Anticipate every possible objection you can and have a persuasive answer in the chamber, locked and loaded.

If you're presenting print work, why not paste the ads into one of the magazines in which they'll be appearing?

If you've done it right and the ads avoid the visual clichés of your category, they should be head and shoulders above the clutter. You don't have to say, "Trust us." You can hand the magazine over to the client and say, "See for yourself."

Never show a client work you don't want them to buy.

I guarantee you, second-rate work is what clients will gravitate to.

The reasoning I have used to allow myself to present so-so ads goes like this: "Well, we gotta sell something to get this campaign going, and time is running out. So we'll present five ads, but we'll make sure they buy only these three great ones. The two so-so ones we'll include just to, you know, help us put on a good presentation. They'll be filler."

But what happens is the client will approve the work they feel safer with, less scared by, and that is almost always the second-rate work.

Conversely, don't leave your best work on the floor at the agency.

"Oh, the client will never buy this." How do you know? They may surprise you. They may not. But don't do their work for them. McElligott once told me, "Go as far as you can. The client will always bring you back."

At the presentation, don't just sit there.

No matter how right your campaign may feel to you, it's not going to magically fly through the client approval process. Even if the client appears to buy it outright, sooner or later they'll start taking potshots. "Little changes" here and there, here and there.

You need to learn to be an articulate defender of your own work. Don't count on your account executive to do it. Don't leave it to your partner. Pay attention in the meeting. Try to understand exactly what may be bothering your client. And then take the initiative to either fix the problem to your satisfaction or come back with the most articulate defense you can.

As you form a defense, your first instincts may be to build a bridge from where you are to where your client is. *("If only I could get them to see how great these ads are.")* Instead, get over to where your client is and build a bridge *back* to your position. With such an attitude, your argument will be more empathetic and more persuasive. You'll be seeing the problem from your client's perspective and they'll know it.

Base your defense on strategy.

Your client is not sitting at his office right now twiddling his thumbs waiting for you to bring in your campaign. A director of marketing for a consumer products company may spend as little as 5 percent of his time on advertising issues—the balance on manufacturing, distribution, financing, and product development. In fact, the managerial strengths that got him to his position in the first place likely had nothing to do with his ability to judge advertising.

Keep this in mind when you go in to present: It isn't a client's job to know great work when they see it. They're generally numbers people.

Copywriter Dick Wasserman put it this way: "Corporate managers are inclined towards understatement. They value calm and quiet, abhor emotional displays, and do everything possible to make decisions in a dispassionate and objective manner. Advertising rubs them the wrong way. It is simply too much like show business for their taste."[3]

To prevail with an audience like this, Alastair Crompton says, "think like a creative person, but talk like an accountant."[4] Don't defend the work on emotional grounds or on the creativity of the execution. Don't say, "This visual is, I'm telling you, it's monstrous. It *kills.*" Instead say, "This visual, as the focus groups bear out, communicates durability." Base your defense on strategy.

You must be able to strategically track, step by step, how you arrived at your campaign. That means having all the relevant product/market/customer facts at your fingertips. There's no such thing as bulletproof, but your ads might be able to dodge a few rounds if you can keep the conversation on strategy alone. After all, that's something the client had a hand in authoring. It's a scary thing to do, but let the work's creativity speak for itself.

Buying creative work is hard. Cut your client some slack.

Before you get angry at a client for not immediately signing off on your brilliant idea, put yourself in his tasseled loafers. It's *hard* buying creative work.

Okay, say we're about to paint the Golden Gate Bridge. It'll cost a million. Which color is right? Gray or blue? Or maybe red? It's a simple question. Come on, what's the right answer?

In a subjective business where there are thirty "right" answers for every problem, deciding which ad to go with is at best a mix of business acumen, gut instinct, second guessing, and a scarecrow in a cornfield pointing down two yellow brick roads.

A few days ago, *I* was the client and I had three of the best creative people in the business showing me ideas for the cover of this book—Bob Barrie, Tom Lichtenheld, and Cabell Harris. Among them, they put fifteen covers on the table, but before the meeting was over I was whining, "Well, I *sort* of like this one, but I was thinking more along these other lines. What if we, what if we . . ."

It's hard. Remember this the next time your work is on the table. Help your client by giving them rational reasons to support what is essentially an emotional decision.

"They might be right."

According to ad myth, Bill Bernbach always carried a little note in his jacket pocket. A note he referred to whenever he was having a disagreement with a client. In small words, one sentence read, "They might be right."

Here's my advice, and it starts a few rungs further down the humility ladder: Always enter into any discussion (with clients, account executives, anybody) with the belief that there is a 50 percent chance you are wrong. I mean, really *believe* in your heart that you could be wrong.

I think that such a belief adds a strong underpinning of persuasiveness to your argument. To the listener, it doesn't feel like you're forcing your opinion on him.

I often think of the analogy of the two kinds of ministers I have seen. A quiet and anonymous minister at a small church who invites me to explore his faith. And the noisy kind I see on TV, sweaty and red-faced, telling me the skin's going to bubble off my soul in Hell if I don't repent now.

Which one is more persuasive to you?

One more thing to consider, again from my old boss, Jerry Della Femina.

Some ad agency people think clients are dumb because they may not know about type, art, illustration, media, the rest of it. Look, how dumb can some guy be when he's managed to build a business that's worth millions? [Many] agencies aren't big businesses. So they ought to have a lot of respect for people smart enough to build big businesses. Remember, success for an agency is a sale in someone's conference room. But clients have to succeed in the open marketplace.[5]

Listening doesn't mean saying yes.

Listen, even when you don't want to. It doesn't cost you anything to listen. It's polite. And even if you think you disagree, by listening you may gather information you can use to put together a more persuasive argument. (As they say: "Diplomacy is the art of saying 'nice doggie' long enough to find a big rock.")

I think our culture portrays passive postures (such as listening) as losing postures. But I think listening can help you kick butt. Relax. Breathe from your stomach. Listen.

Choose your battles carefully.

No matter how carefully you prepare your work, no matter how impeccable you are about covering every base, crossing every *t*, dotting every *i*, the red pencil's gonna come out. Clients are going to mess with your visual and change your copy.

H. G. Wells wrote, "No passion in the world is equal to the passion to alter someone's draft."

We need to pause here for a minute so I can make this point as clear to you as I am able. It's an important one.

Millions of years of evolution have wired a network of biological certainties into the human organism. There is the need to eat. There is the need to sleep. And then, right before the need to procreate, is the client need to *change* every ad his agency shows him. This need is spinal. Nothing you can do or say, no facts you lay down, no prayers you send up, will stop a client from diddling with your concept. It's something you need to accept as reality early in your career.

It didn't start with you and it'll still be going on when some Detroit agency takes in the campaign for the new antigravity cars. The fact is, we're in a subjective industry—partly business and partly art. Everybody is going to have an opinion. It's just that the clients have paid for the right to have their opinion. Advertising, ultimately, is a service industry.

Consider the drawing reprinted here (Fig. 9.2): a client making changes to an ad as a frustrated copywriter looks on. I found it in a book called *Confessions of a Copywriter*, published in 1930 by the Dartnell Corporation. That date again—nineteen *thirty*.

Figure 9.2   Except for the clothes, this 1930 engraving of a client changing a writer's copy looks like it could have happened yesterday. © Reprinted with permission of Dartnell Corporation.

They were doing it then and I suspect they've been doing it since earliest recorded history. I have this image of a client in Egypt, 3,000 years before Christ, looking at some hieroglyphs on the walls of the Pyramids, saying, "I think instead of " 𓂀𓏏𓈖𓅱𓆼𓇳 ," we should say, " 𓇳𓅱𓂋𓏏𓈖 ."

Get used to it. Even some of the writing on this page about rewriting was rewritten by my publisher's editor. Nothing is safe.

I say, if they want to mess around with your body copy, let them. If they want to change the colors from red to green, let them. Any hieroglyphs they want to change, let them. Protect the *pyramid.* If you get out of there with the big idea intact, consider yourself a genius.

Tom Monahan says, "[Squabbling over body copy and other details are] not where the advertising battles are won. Ideas—big, differentiating, selling ideas—are what win. And anything that takes away even an ounce of energy from the creating or selling of those ideas is misdirected effort."[6]

The moral: Don't win every battle and lose the war.

RESEARCH: BE AFRAID. BE VERY AFRAID.

Research isn't science.

Here's how advertising works: You toil for weeks to come up with a good solution to your client's problem. Then your campaign is taken to an anonymous building on the outskirts of town and shown to a "focus group"—people who've been stopped on the street the previous week, identified as target customers, and paid a small amount of money for their opinion.

After a long day working at their jobs, these tired pedestrians arrive at the research facility and are led into a small room without windows or hope. In this barren, forlorn little box, they are shown your work in its half-formed state while you and the client watch through a two-way mirror.

Here's the amazing part. These people all turn out to be advertising *experts* with piercing insights on why every ad shown them should be force-fed into the nearest shredder fast enough to choke the chopping blades.

Yet who can blame them? They've been watching TV since they were kids and have been bored by 100,000 hours of very, very bad commercials. Now it's payback time, Mr. Madison Avenue Suspenders Man. And because they're seeing mere storyboards they think, wow, we get to kill the beast *and* crush its eggs.

Meanwhile, in the room behind the mirror, the client turns to you and says, "Looks like you're workin' the weekend, idea boy."

Welcome to advertising.

A committee, it has been said, is a cul-de-sac down which ideas are lured and quietly strangled. The same can be said for the committee's cousin, the focus group. But this research process, however wildly capricious and unscientific, is here to stay.

Clients are used to testing. They test their products. They test locations for their stores. They test the new flavor, the packaging, and the name on the top. And much of this testing pays off. So don't think they're going to spend a couple of million dollars airing a commercial based solely on your sage advice: "Hey, business dudes, I think this spot rocks."

Used correctly, research is great. What better way is there to get inside the customer's head? To be what Marshall McLuhan called the "frog men of the mind" and find out what people like and don't like, to understand how they live. There is no better way. Most of the good research isn't done in little buildings outside of town either, but right downtown in the bars, asking drinkers about their favorite booze; asking shoppers how they choose a product; eavesdropping on real people as they talk about a category or a brand.

The point is, the best people in the business use research to generate ideas, not to judge them. They use it at the beginning of the whole advertising process to find out what to say. When it's used to determine how to say it, great ideas suffer horribly.

Should your work suffer at the hands of a focus group, and it will, there isn't much you can do except appeal to the better angels of your client's nature.

What follows are some arguments against the reading of sheep entrails. Or the subjective science of copy testing.

Ninety-nine percent of creative people agree: Testing storyboards doesn't work.

Testing, by its very nature, looks for what is wrong with a commercial, not what is right. Look hard enough for something wrong and you'll sure enough find it. (I could stare at a picture of Miss November and in a half hour I'd start to notice, is that some broccoli in her teeth? Look, right there between the lateral incisor and the left canine, see?)

Testing assumes people react intellectually to commercials, that people watching TV in their living rooms dissect and analyze these interruptions to their sitcoms. (*"Honey, come in here. I think these*

TV people are forwarding an argument that doesn't track logically. Bring a pen and paper.") In reality, you and I both know their reactions are visceral and instantaneous.

Testing is inaccurate because storyboards don't have the magic of finished commercials. Would a focus group approve this copy? "You ain't nothin' but a hound dog. Cryin' all the time. You ain't nothin' but a hound dog. Cryin' all the time. You ain't never caught a rabbit and you ain't no friend of mine." Probably not. (I can just see a group member putting down his doughnut to protest. "Why are you calling me a dog? Do I smell?") But sung by Elvis, people just like the ones in focus groups bought copies of "Hound Dog" by the millions.

Testing rewards commercials that are vague and fuzzy because vague-and-fuzzy doesn't challenge the viewer.

Testing rewards commercials that are derivative because commercials that have a familiar feel score better than commercials that are unique, strange, odd, or new. The very qualities that can lift a finished commercial above the television clutter.

If tone is important to a client, testing is inaccurate because 12 colored pictures pasted to a board will never communicate tone like actual film footage, voice-over, and music.

Testing, no matter how well disguised, asks consumers to be advertising experts. And invariably they feel obligated to prove it.

Finally, testing assumes we really know what makes a commercial work and that it can be quantifiably analyzed. It can't. Not in my opinion. It's impossible to measure a live snake.

Bill Bernbach said, "We are so busy measuring public opinion, we forget we can mold it. We are so busy listening to statistics that we forget we can create them." This simple truth about advertising is lost the minute a focus group sits down to do its business. In those small rooms, the power of advertising to affect behavior is not only subverted, it's reversed. The dynamic of a commercial coming *out* of the television *to* consumers is replaced with consumers telling the commercial what to say.

I say, big deal if a group says your storyboard doesn't reflect their opinions. With a good director and a couple of airings on the right programs, their opinions may reflect your commercial's.

These arguments, for what they are worth, might come in handy someday, especially if you have a client who likes the commercial you propose, but has to defend poor test scores to a management committee.

Extensive research has proven that extensive research is often wrong.

From a book called *Radio Advertising* by Bob Schulberg, I bring this research study to your attention:

> J. Walter Thompson did recall studies on commercials that ran during a heavily-viewed mini-series, "The Winds of War." The survey showed that 19 percent of the respondents recalled Volkswagen commercials; 32 percent, Kodak; 32 percent, Prudential; 28 percent American Express; and 16 percent Mobil Oil. The catch is that none of these companies advertised on "The Winds of War."[7]

In the mid-'80s, research told management of the Coca-Cola Company that younger people preferred a sweeter, more Pepsi-like taste. Overlooking fierce customer loyalty to this century-old battleship of a brand, they reformulated Coca-Cola into New Coke, and in the process packed about $1 billion down a rat hole.

"We forget we can mold it."

Research people told writer Hal Riney that entering the wine cooler category was a big mistake. Seagram's and California Cooler had it locked up. Then Riney began running his Bartles & Jaymes commercials and a year later his client had the #1-selling wine cooler in America.

"We forget we can mold it."

Research people told writer Cliff Freeman when he was working on Wendy's hamburgers, "Under absolutely *no* circumstances run 'Where's the Beef?'" After it ran, sales shot up 25 percent for the year and Wendy's moved from fifth to third place in fast-food sales. The 20,000 newspaper articles lauding the commercial didn't hurt either.

"We forget we can mold it."

And what some call the greatest campaign of the twentieth century, Volkswagen—none of it was subjected to pretesting. The man who helped produce that Volkswagen campaign had a saying: "We are so busy measuring public opinion, we forget we can mold it."

Because focus groups can prove anything, do they prove anything?

British ad star Tim Delaney, in a famous article on the value of intuition, wrote:

> Have you noticed what happens when five agencies are competing for an account? They all come up with completely different strategies and ideas—and yet, miraculously, each of them is able to prove, through objective research, that their solution is the right one. If nothing else does, this alone should devalue the currency of focus groups. . . . Researchers think that if you spend a lot of time analyzing a problem beforehand, it will bring you closer to the advertising solution. But the truth is, you only really begin to crack advertising problems as you get deeper and deeper into the writing. You just have to sit down and start writing on some kind of pretext—and that initiates the flow of ideas that eventually brings a solution. In [my] agency, we start writing as early as possible, before the researchers have done their analysis. And we usually find that the researchers are always trailing behind us, telling us things we've already thought of.[8]

The writing itself is the solution to the problem. It's in the writing itself that the answers appear, when you're in there getting your hands dirty mucking about in the mud of the client's marketing reality. The answers are right there in that place where there's direct contact between the patient and the doctor. And if the doctor has a question about how to proceed, who would you want him to ask for advice? A focus group of grocers, lawyers, and cab drivers? Personally, I'd want it to be another doctor.

I have a friend who walks around the agency trying to find out if a concept he's done is any good. He keeps going around until the "It's cool" votes outnumber the "It sucks." Sometimes he doesn't get the answer he wants and keeps working.

You know what? In my opinion, it's the only pretesting that works. The agency hallway.

PROTECTING YOUR WORK

Well, so much for research. If your concept manages to limp out of the focus groups alive, congratulations.

But even if your idea fares well in tests, if it's new and unusual the client is *still* likely to squirm. As scientist W. I. Beveridge noted, "The human mind likes a strange idea as little as the body likes a strange protein and resists it with a similar energy."

Even if they like your idea, they'll begin suggesting "minor changes." The Chinese call this "The Death of a Thousand Cuts." Minor changes kill great ads, very slowly and with incredible pain. By the time they've inflicted their thousandth minor change, you and your ad will both be begging for a swift bullet to the head.

Sometimes you're going to need to deliver that bullet yourself. If client changes have hurt your original idea, pull the trigger. You think it's hard to look at your "fixed" ad on a layout pad? Wait till you see it as a spread in *Time* magazine.

Over the years, I've heard clients bring up the same minor changes time and again. Here are a few of them.

Your client asks that you feature more than one product or benefit.

Clients often ask for an ad to tout their full line of fine products. Who can blame them? The page they're buying seems roomy enough to throw in five or six more things besides your snappy little idea, doesn't it? But full-line ads are effective only as magazine thickener, nothing else.

The reason is simple. Customers never go shopping for full lines of products. I don't. Do you? (*"Honey, start the car. We're going to the mall to buy everything."*) Customers have specific needs. It stands to reason that ads addressing specific needs are more effective.

Smart companies know this. Coca-Cola owns nearly 80 brands of soft drinks, but they've never run an ad for all of them with some catch-all claim like, "Bubbly, sugar-based liquids in a variety of vastly different tastes for all your thirst needs."

If your client says he has three important things to say, tell the account executive the client needs three ads.

If that doesn't work, perhaps you'll just have to convince your client that there's a certain part of the audience that he's just not going to reach. Filling his ad with extraneous claims or peripheral products may attract some of this fringe audience, but the dilution will be at the cost of the main audience he needs most.

It's this simple: You can't pound in a nail that's lying on its side.

A client says "Negative headlines are wrong."

Well, you can start by pointing out that what he just said was negative but communicated his position quite respectably. But there are some other rebuttals you can try.

Take a look at the photograph reprinted here (Fig. 9.3). It's a very positive image, isn't it? There's happiness and cheerful camaraderie all around, and everybody's enjoying the client's fine product. It's also so boring I want to *saw off my right foot* just so I can feel something, feel anything.

It's boring because there is no tension in the picture. No question left unanswered. No story. No drama. And consequently, no interest.

Perhaps you could begin by explaining to your client that one of the basic tenets of drama (and we are indeed in the business of dramatizing the benefits of our clients' products) is conflict. The bad guy (competition) moseys into town, kicks open the saloon door, and Cowboy Bob (your client) looks up from his card game.

Conflict = drama = interest. Without it, you have no story to tell. No friction between the tire and the road. No beginning, middle, or end. And consequently, no interest.

"Humorists have always made trouble pay," said E. B. White.

The brutal truth is that people don't slow down to look at the highway, they slow down to look at the highway accident. Maybe we're ashamed to admit that, but it is riveting—trouble and conflict always are. You'll never see a newspaper headline that reads: "Plane lands safely at airport."

The thing to remember about trouble and conflict in a commercial is this: As long as your client's product is ultimately portrayed in a positive light or is seen to solve a customer problem, the net return is positive.

As Tom Monahan pointed out, "The true communication isn't what you say. It's what the receiver takes away."[9]

Here are some other arguments you might try on an intransigent client.

Remind your client that one of the biggest success stories in market-

Figure 9.3   Q: "Why can't you do something positive?" A: This is why.

ing textbooks is Federal Express, a tiny outfit in Memphis that became an international commodity. This company owes its success almost entirely to a series of television commercials featuring terrible conflict; things going wrong, packages arriving late, nitwits getting fired.

Tell your client about a small classified ad that ran in 1900. (This is another story stolen from Neil French.) The ad read, "Men wanted for Hazardous Journey. Small wages, bitter cold, long months of complete darkness, constant danger, safe return doubtful. Honor and recognition in case of success—Ernest Shackleton."

When the famous explorer placed this ad looking for fellow adventurers to trek with him in search of the South Pole, he received many responses. Should it instead have read "Happy snow bunnies needed for Popsicle Party"? Probably not. It worked because readers were piqued by the honesty of the ad and the challenge of the imminent journey.

If that doesn't convince your client, try this one from copywriter Jim Durfee: "Would you call the following statement positive or negative: 'Don't step back or you'll fall off the cliff.' "

Negatives have power. Try writing the Ten Commandments positively. If you did, I bet it wouldn't fit on two stone tablets anymore.

Negatives are a linguistic construction we're all familiar with, one we've been hearing since we were caught dangling the cat over the baby. They're neither good nor bad, merely an executional detail.

So try to keep your client from focusing on the details. It isn't the details customers remember anyway. If you look at most day-after testing results, you'll find that customers may not remember a single word of a commercial. Just the main idea and what's good about the product, which is all that matters.

A client says, "Our competitors could run that same ad!"

They'll usually go on to say, "If you cover up our logo, this could be the other guys' ad."

"We said it first" is the simple answer. "Their logo isn't down there. Yours is."

Sometimes clients need to be reminded that their product isn't substantially different from the competition's. All that may distinguish the two is the advertising you propose. Nothing else.

Your client needs to see that while there's no explicit claim in the ad different from what his competitor might be able to say, the ad and its execution have many implicit messages the client can call his own. Be it the concept, the tone, the look of the campaign; together they are giving the client a personality like no other.

Don't force your hand, though. If you can get the client to find in their product a unique selling proposition, all the better. Agree to start over if any significant difference can be found.

If not, you need to get your client to see that execution can be content and that personality can be proprietary. They're called "preemptive claims"—claims any competitor could've made had they moved fast enough. Your client may see that it's simply a matter of which company's going to get first dibs on the ground staked out by your concept.

It comes down to "We were here first."

As Wasserman notes, it could've just as easily been "Winston Country." But Marlboro got there first.

A client asks you to print their phone number in big, bold type.

Ask if they'd also like to have their number shouted in radio spots. Will people be more likely to call the number if we scream it at them? No? Then why do it in print?

Picture this: A woman (man) at a bar, slides a folded matchbook across the mahogany and under your napkin. You open it and see a phone number. Are you more likely to call if the number is written in inch-thick numerals with a fat red crayon? Of course not.

Yes, the phone number should be in there, probably in the last sentence or maybe by the logo. But advise the client that transmogrifying the type so you can needlessly shriek a phone number is not only desperate and without class, it adds yet another element to a crowded space and can only hurt the look of an ad.

If the reader wants your phone number after seeing the ad, he'll get it. From the ad, from the phone book, or from 4-1-1—somehow he'll get it.

Your client wants the phone number read three times in every radio spot.

Formula dictates the ol' "That number again, . . ." but common sense suggests this is nonsense.

Ask your client: Have you ever been in the car and on hearing a phone number in a commercial, cut across two lanes, slowed down, stopped, dug out a pencil, and jotted down a number? I've never written down a number from a commercial I've heard at *home* sitting at my desk with a big, fat bucket of freshly sharpened pencils at my elbow.

I still think you should include one mention of the number. But not because I think listeners will write it down. What a phone number says is the client is accessible, that they're in the book or at 4-1-1. You can *call* them.

Your client tries to "personalize" your ad with that "Hey, Minneapolis . . ." kind of thing.

Personally I find this kind of talk patronizing. Like when a car salesman panders to me by using my name too many times in a sentence. "You know, Luke, it may just be me, Luke, but I *see* you in this car. I really do, Luke." I find it overly familiar and transparent.

People hate being targeted for a sale. They hate being marketed to. Hate being known quantities. As in those irritating headlines that begin, "And *you* thought that . . ."

Or worse, "You. You're a woman on the go. You have a baby in one arm and a briefcase in the other." I watch commercials like that and I say, "Hey, I'm a *guy*. And I'm not 'on the go.' I happen to be at home in my underwear and I have a bag of Krispee Orange Cheese Deals in one hand and a remote in the other and you are *outta* here, pigweed." Zap.

Just say what your benefit is and let it go. Self-consciously customizing your message around some pinpointed demographic adds nothing to the persuasiveness of an idea and may just get you zapped.

To get trout, fishermen fish where trout are and use lures trout like. They don't have little signs next to the lures saying, "You're swimmin' upstream, you're breathin' underwater. This is *your* kind of lure, isn't it, fish boy?"

A client asks, "Why are you wasting 25 seconds of my TV spot entertaining people?"

Other ways clients ask this is, "Can we mention the product sooner?" or "Can't we just get to the point?"

This is a client who mistakenly believes that people watch television to see his commercial. (*"Honey, get in here! The commercial's almost on!"*)

There is no entitlement to the customer's attention. It is earned.

And make no mistake, we're not starting from zero with customers. Thanks to Whipple, Snuggles, and Ring Around the Collar, we're starting at less than zero. There is a high wall around every customer. And every day another brick is added.

You need to get your client to see that those 25 seconds of "wasted" time in the commercial are his ticket through the gate. You're not welcome until customers like you. And they won't like you until they listen to you. And they won't listen to you if you open your pitch with bulleted copy points of your product's superiority.

To visit the door-to-door salesman analogy again, you can't just dispense with knocking on the door. Clients who say, "Let's lose all that entertainment stuff" are really saying, "Forget the introducing ourselves at the door. Forget that doorbell crap, too. In fact, let's just jimmy the lock with a brochure and barge into their kitchen with a fistful of facts. We'll *make* 'em listen."

You can't. You're not welcome until they like you. Ring the doorbell and straighten your tie.

Your client takes your concept literally.

This is a hard one.

Let's use one of Cliff Freeman's hilarious Little Caesar's pizza spots as an example (Fig. 9.4), the one featuring the famous "stretchy cheese." In these spots, goofy-looking customers pull slices of pizza out of the box and attempt to carry them away to their supper table. The cheese, connecting the slice with the pizza still in the box, stretches like a rubber band, snaps them back, usually causing some sort of cartoon injury along the way.

"Well, I don't know," says the client. "Our cheese doesn't really stretch that far. And if it never breaks, doesn't that mean it's kind of rubbery?"

The client is taking the storyboard literally. It would be pleasant if simply pointing that out would make the client say, "Oh, my mistake. By all means, produce the spots." This is known as a hallucination.

What the client needs is someone to shift his paradigm so that he can see the commercial as a TV viewer does and not as the product manager of a large corporation.

But first, back him up.

Is it agreed that the job of advertising is to dramatize the benefit of the product? (In this case, the extra helpings of cheese.) Not show the benefit, dramatize the benefit. If showing the benefit is the goal, we need only to picture someone holding a slice of pizza and saying, "Look at all this extra cheese. Now *that's* value." We could also throw our money down the middle hole of an outhouse and achieve the same effect, since no one will watch or remember Smiley Pizza Man.

So it's agreed that dramatizing the benefit is our goal?

"Yes, but the cheese never breaks," says the client. "Maybe the stretching part is funny, but rubbery cheese is no good. I'm telling you, I've been in food services for 15 years and I've watched focus groups and heard customers *say* those very words."

Here's where the client needs to take a leap of faith. Take his hand. Lean out over the precipice and tell him this: "In TV Land, the rules are different."

Figure 9.4   A Little Caesar's customer boards a plane carrying pizza trailing stretchy cheese. Out in TV Land, nobody wondered, "Gosh, if their cheese stretches that much, isn't it rubbery? Let's go to Domino's instead."

And jump.

The rules of acceptable logic are different in TV Land. Viewers not only know the rules are different, they *expect* them to be. If the rules aren't different they might as well be watching the news. TV Land is not reality. It is entertainment. Television is watched by tired people needing escape from reality.

In reality, cops don't catch the bad guy. In TV Land, they do. In reality, coyotes kill roadrunners. In TV Land, coyotes end up under the big Acme® brand anvil.

And while rubbery cheese isn't appetizing in reality, in TV Land the comic device of stretchy cheese that's both rubbery *and* delicious is perfectly acceptable logic. The device, one the viewer tacitly knows is created for entertainment, transcends all reality-based concerns about edibility, leapfrogs all taste issues of rubbery/nonrubbery cheese, and lands with a big welcome splash in the mind of the customer with its intended message—this pizza has lots of yummy cheese.

The rules are different in TV but they're still rules. You must obey them as long as you wish to retain the attention of your audience. Stretchy cheese, rubber logic, and other dramatic devices are the accepted currency in TV Land. They are the only way to communicate what is often a bland corporate message.

In fact, that rubbery cartoon cheese *is* a bland corporate message (*"Our pizza has more cheese"*), but one that's seen through the funhouse prisms of TV Land. At a certain level, all corporate messages that show up in TV Land are bland because they weren't invited. In order to come to the table, the ante is entertainment.

But the chasm between the cool fluorescent lights of America's corporate meeting rooms and the play-school colors of TV entertainment is deep and wide. It takes a client who's either imaginative or brave to make the leap. Clearly, Little Caesar's is both.

In a wonderful book for clients called *That's Our New Ad Campaign?*, Dick Wasserman takes on this issue:

> When [clients] evaluate advertising executions, they do not understand that consumers react to ads in a generalized, unanalytical, emotional way. . . . Consumers are much more imaginative than many advertisers are willing to give them credit for. Readers and viewers do not have to be led by the hand to understand what a client's advertising is getting at. All they need is a couple of key verbal and visual guideposts, and they are quite capable of filling in the blanks.[10]

Your client will be uncomfortable in TV Land. Once you get back to the safety of the conference room, you need to convince him that the literal approach is actually riskier than obeying the wacky rules of TV. A literal approach, where you simply tell the client's story is, as Wasserman says, a speech; what viewers want is a play.

Your client may be agreeing with you at this point, but he's not going to like it. He's going to be like that one guy in every disaster movie, up to his knees in floodwater but still checking his hair in the mirror. He is out of his element.

Remind him his discomfort is natural. This isn't Wall Street. But it isn't Sesame Street, either. It's the intersection—that place where the odd bedfellows of business and advertising meet. The corner of Art and Commerce.

Bill Bernbach was perhaps talking to this same kind of client when he said: "Is creativity some obscure, esoteric art form? Not on your life. It's the most practical thing a businessman can employ."[11]

Your client asks, "Why do you have to cast such goofy-looking characters for my TV spot?"

We're talking about those concepts where some kind of nerd or schmuck or victim is key to the execution, not those spots where a normal-looking everyday Joe will suffice.

When a client has a problem with the casting it's usually because they're taking the commercial literally. Often at the root of it is a fear that your commercial is making fun of his customers.

Some clients seem to think their customers can't relate to anyone that doesn't look like them. (I'm tempted to ask, "Then why are you wearing a suit you first saw in a store window worn by a brainless, bald-headed mannequin?" A workable analogy, but probably not a good idea.)

You need to convince them that the same rules of TV Land apply to the actors in commercials.

To be even allowed into TV Land and welcomed into America's living rooms, your characters must have some scratch, something about them that's funny or unusual. Viewers are either bored by or secretly angry at nice-looking models with good haircuts. (Or "AMWs," as they're called in Los Angeles—actress, model, whatever.)

Tell your client that viewers weren't offended by that slightly overweight geek who was knocked around the room by the pizza with stretchy cheese.

Viewers weren't offended by the jacklegs, yes-men, and bootlicks that made up Federal Express's confederacy of dunces. The late Patrick Kelly, who wrote the FedEx spots, said, "People identify with the schlemiel. We've all been that way at one time or another. . . . The identification comes on a subconscious level. At the *conscious* level, we see the idiot as someone else."[12]

What will offend viewers is having their sitcom or football game interrupted by a cheerful Stepford Wife lip-reading a cue card full of benefits. They want to be en-ter-*tained*.

Your client needs to be reminded that when it comes to mass communication, all customers are smart. Even a mouth-breather in a trailer park watching commercials on a stolen TV set with tinfoil on the antenna knows the rules of TV Land. He was raised on them.

And, if the truth be known, there are a lot of funny-looking people out there in Real-Life Land.

Your client says (as the law requires them to), "Can you make the logo bigger?"

Clients are about their logos like guys are about their . . . you know.

They love talking about them. They love to look at them. They want you to look at them. They think the bigger they are, the more effective they are. And they try to sneak looks at other guy's logos when they can.

But as any woman will tell you, nobody cares.

Just the same, when you swagger into a client's boardroom with a full-page newspaper ad punctuated by a logo you could cover with a dime, fur's gonna fly.

I remember we had one client who called the agency, very angry. He had just seen an outdoor board our agency had done for his company and he couldn't see the logo very well.

"Uh-oh," said the account executive who fielded the call. "Where did you see this billboard?"

From a plane.

The client was angry because he couldn't see his logo from a *plane* as it circled La Guardia airport.

But let's back up a little. If your client has a problem with the size of the logo, ask him first, "Do you agree the ad is good? Is it strategically correct and creatively memorable?" It is?

If it's agreed the ad successfully stops a reader and engages him with an offer that intrigues, what do you suppose the reader will look for next? It's doubtful he'll look at the logo of some other ad. It's doubtful he'll take his attention off the leash and let it wander into the park like a stray dog. There's a *dynamic* involved here. The reader's just seen something he wants. Where can he get it? The logo. Unless you're using a watermark, the reader will almost certainly find it, no matter what its size.

"But why can't you just make it a little bigger? What does it hurt?"

It's a matter of taste. The Latin saying is "*Degustibus non est disputandum.*" Taste cannot be disputed. But, forget Cicero; let's dispute.

In every ad there are explicit and implicit messages, both equally important. The explicit message is what the headline and visual are saying. But implicitly, the layout of the ad is sending many messages about the quality of the product, about the class, the demeanor, the personality of your client. They are all subtle. And while explicit messages can sometimes be adjusted with a wrench, implicit messages need an expert's touch.

Your client needs to know that the art director's decision about the size of the logo was made after careful consideration of these implicit messages. Too much logo and the ad becomes a used-car salesman. Increase the size of the logo a little more and the lapels on his suit become wider; increase it again and the plaid of his coat becomes louder.

The biggest logo I've ever seen towered 20 stories over Times Square: a giant Prudential logo, easily 30 yards square. No sales message, no headline, just yards and yards of blue logo. When a person looks up and sees this giant logo, what is he to do with the information? Would it be more relevant or more persuasive if it were 50 yards square? Ooooh, what if we made it one *hundred* yards square?

Where is it written that large logos increase sales? When introducing yourself, do you say your name in a booming voice? "Hi, my name is **Bob Johnson!**" Do the large bottles of Coke with bigger logos sell faster than the cans? Are your business cards the size of welcome mats? If cattlemen heated immense brands and seared the entire *sides* of cows, would fewer be rustled?

Ads without any logos at all are often the most powerful. Clients aren't likely to buy this argument but it's valid nevertheless. A logo says, "I'm an ad!" and an ad says, "Turn the page!" But an intriguing message without any logo to defuse it can be a riveting interruption to a magazine. It doesn't say "This message brought to you by . . ." It says, "This message." Some of the most effective ads I've ever seen worked without the benefit of a logo. Three of them are in this book.

The reason they worked is that customers don't buy company logos. They buy *benefits.* If an ad successfully communicates benefit, logo size is relevant only in terms of quality of design, something best left to the art director's well-trained eye—his intuition.

Find a way to give the client a gentle reminder that this intangible thing, this intuition, is our business. Ask him if he would presume to tell his doctor what the diagnosis should be and what prescription to write. Or if he would instruct his lawyer in the nuances of contract law. I know *I* wouldn't.

I won't even tell the trashman not to lift the garbage can with his back. I figure he knows what he's doing.

Your client gets a few letters from "offended" customers and pulls the campaign.

Many clients worry that their ad may offend somebody somewhere. And they begin yanking commercials off the air after they receive one or two phone calls about the commercial. Or they begin telling their ad agencies to write everything in such a way that not one soul in a country of 250 million will find a scintilla of impropriety.

This is advertising by terrorism, pure and simple. The marketing plan to the many is overruled by the pious sensibilities of the few. It is a form of "political correctness," which is itself a politically correct word for fascism. It may be Fascism Lite, but it's still book burning, only we're burning them one adjective, one headline, and one script at a time.

Don't give in. Tell the truth and run.

In the next ad you craft, say what you think is the right thing. Remember, your job is to sell the client's wares to as many people as you can. To appeal to the masses, not the minority. Tell the truth and run. And let the chronically offended pen their lugubrious letters. Let them whine.

The trick will be to get your client to see what a quark-size minority these kleenex-dabbing, career whiners are. The way I put it: "The letter flooded in." Hey, it's a *letter,* not Omaha Beach.

I say: B-F-D. The letter flooded in. Fine. Even if it's 100 letters, big deal. Smart clients know they'll get angry letters just for hanging out their shingle. You build a factory, you get a letter. Sell a product, get a letter. I'll wager you could publish the cure for AIDS in tomorrow's paper and by Friday you'll get a missive scribbled in crayon on the back of a Burger King place mat from someone sniveling, "Why didn't you cure cancer *first?*"

Advise your client to run the ad. The world, amazingly, will not stop, because 99.99 percent of the people who see the ad will somehow manage to get on with their lives. The other .01 percent will turn down the volume of whatever wrestling show they're watching and reach for the nearest #10 envelope. Fine. Let them mewl.

To soften the ad in advance or to pull the ad once it's run is to surrender your company's marketing to a consumer group you could fit in a phone booth—an angry clutch of stamp-licking busybodies with nothing better to do than peruse *Redbook* magazine looking for imagined slights to their piety. Ask your client, "Do you want your company being run out of a church basement? Do you want to give every pursed-lipped, pen-wielding, moral policeman with a roll of stamps free rein to sit on your board of directors and dictate marketing plans?"

Tell your client these people are the minority. That's the fraction with the "1" above the line and the really *big* number on the bottom. And this is America. Where the Constitution says in so many big, fancy words, "What the majority says, *goes.*"

Outlast the client.

I hope that having one or two of these counterarguments tucked away in your quiver helps you save an ad one day. But the reality of this business is that sometimes nothing you can do or say is going to pull an ad out of the fire. If a client doesn't like it, it's going to die.

The reasons clients have for not liking an ad often defy analysis. I once saw a client kill an ad because it pictured a blue flyswatter. Why the client killed it, he wouldn't say. "Just consider it dead." When pressed for an explanation months later, he implied that he'd had a "bad experience" with a blue flyswatter as a child. The room grew quiet and we changed the subject.

Ads die sometimes for reasons that have nothing to do with the ad. I heard this story from a friend in the business. His agency had put on a big presentation to a large group of distributors. It had gone poorly; everything died. After the meeting, the creative director was out in the lobby of the hotel, trying to figure out what had gone wrong. "I showed you the strategy months ago," he said to the most influential member of the group. "I showed you the research results. How could you not like it?"

"Son," he said, "we can do whatever we want."

The CD protests, "But that's unfair."

"You simply don't understand, young man," said the leader. "There are 44 millionaires in that room . . . and you're not one of them."

So get ready for it. All is not lost though. You have one last weapon in your arsenal: persistence. I once read that the definition of success is simply getting up one more time than you fall.

To that end, I urge you to simply outlast the client. I don't mean by digging in your heels, but by rolling around and past their resistance like a stream around a rock. I once did 13 campaigns on one assignment for a very difficult client. Thirteen different campaigns over the period of a *year* and each one was killed for increasingly irrational reasons. But each campaign we came back with was good.

They kept killing them, but they killed the campaign only 13 times. The thing is, we presented 14.

There's always another ad.

Instead of fighting, here's another idea. After you come up with an idea, do what Mark Fenske told me. "Pat it on the rear and say 'Good luck, little buddy' and send it on its way." Mark believes you shouldn't make a career of protecting work. This thought runs counter to these last couple of pages, but maybe he's right. Mark says just come up with an idea and then walk away; there's going to be another opportunity to do a great ad tomorrow. Not a bad idea. Mark may outlive us all.

Remember who the enemy is.

Lest these last few pages give the impression I think the client is the enemy, they're not. Remember, the enemy is the client's competition. The other guys across town with the scummy overpriced products. But as in any marriage, there are going to be arguments with your client. Unlike marriage, in advertising you can actually win some.

PICKING UP THE PIECES

Don't lose vigilance when work is approved.

Sometimes when I have sold an ad I didn't think would ever sell, I become so happy I lose my critical faculties and blithely allow the ad to go off into production unescorted. I forget to keep sweating the details.

Moral: Don't fumble in the end zone.

Don't get depressed when work is killed.

The ads you come back with are usually better. And when you're feeling down in the dumps, remember, nothing gets you back on your feet faster than a great campaign.

Sometimes the playing field changes when a campaign is killed. For one thing, you know more now about what the client wants. Also, you'll probably be left with a shorter deadline. A curse, but a blessing, too. A time crunch may force a client to buy your next campaign. If the media's been bought, they may have to buy your idea. So make it great.

A short deadline also has remarkable motivating properties. Someone once told me the best amphetamine is a ticking clock.

If they don't buy number two or three or four, hang in there. The highs in the business are very high and the lows very low. Learn not to take either one too seriously.

James Michener once observed, "Character consists of what you do on the third and fourth tries."

After you've totaled a car, you can still salvage stuff out of the trunk.

Okay, so the client killed everything. (I actually had an account executive come back from a meeting and say, "They approved the *size* of the ads!" Yay.) But you know what? You can still get something out of the deal.

If you're part of the presentation, you can at least improve your relationship with the client. I don't think there's any client who actually enjoys killing work. Ask any creative director; it's easier to say yes and avoid the confrontation. They know you've worked hard on it. But remember, they're not completely without insight into what sells their product.

If you can take the loss like a professional and still sit there and be your same funny self and ask, okay, so what the hell *do* you want, you can build rapport. They're going to like you for it. And they're going to trust you more the second time around.

Even if your work is killed, produce it.

This is another piece of advice from Mark Fenske. If you're working at an agency where most of your stuff is fed to the Foam Core furnace, you need to begin worrying now what you're going to show at your next interview. *("Well, see, the client really sucked and they made me do this one. . . . And this one, too. . . . Yeah, but I had this other idea, no really, you shoulda seen it, . . . Hey, why are we walking towards the elevators?")* If you can somehow get to tight layouts, even on the dead ads, at least you'll have something to show a prospective CD what you're capable of.

If you're not producing agency work, do freelance.

This is dicey advice. Some agencies don't like it. They figured they invited you to the dance, you should dance with them.

But you do have to watch out for yourself. You need to keep adding to your portfolio. So if you find yourself in an agency that's producing only meeting fodder, foam core, and rewrites, maybe it's fair to flirt with a small client who needs a few ads.

Doing the occasional freelance campaign will not only keep your book fresh, it can keep your hopes alive, keep you excited about the possibilities of this business.

Keep a file of great dead ideas.

I've referred back to mine many times and have reanimated lots of old ideas, sometimes for the same client that originally killed them. I know many creative people who do all their writing in big, fat blank books that they put on the shelf when the books are full. Nothing gets thrown away. Except by clients.

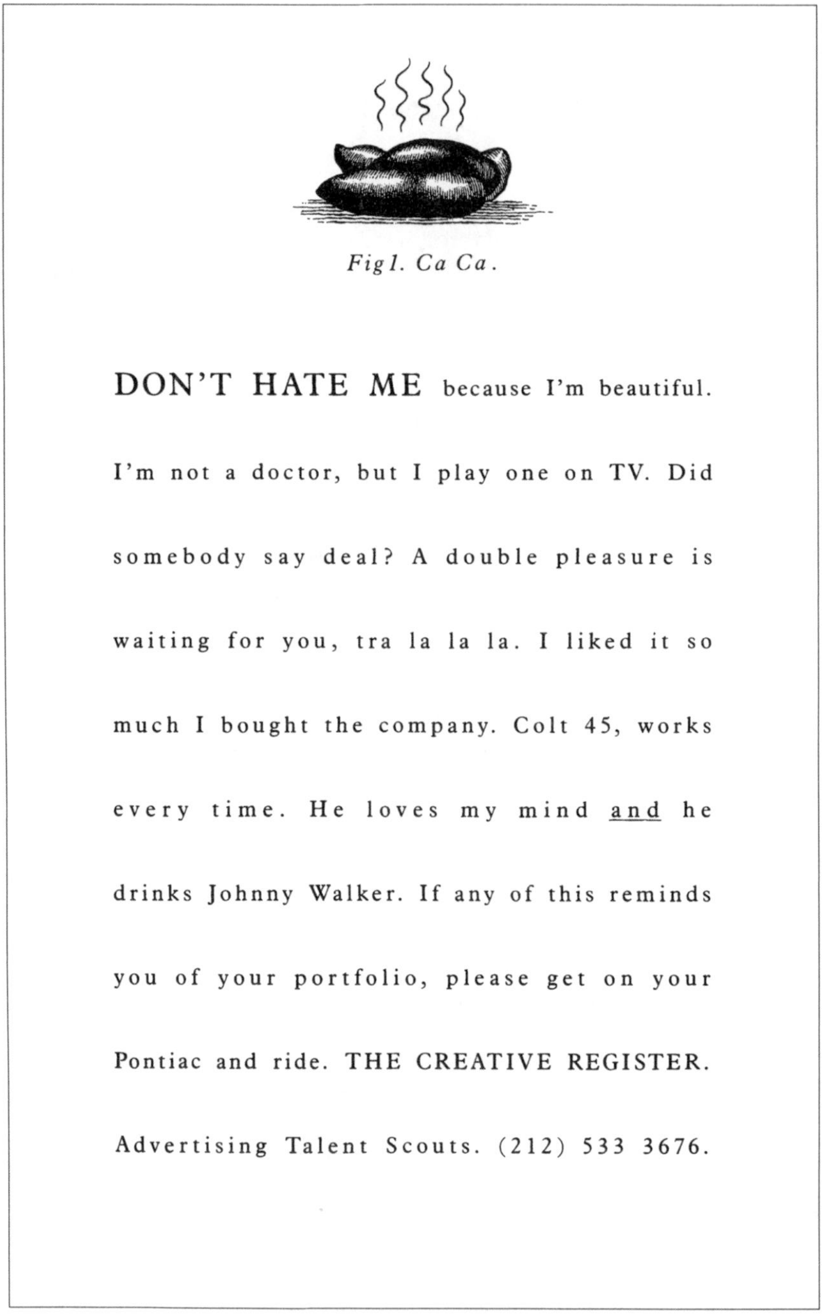

Fig 1. Ca Ca.

DON'T HATE ME because I'm beautiful.

I'm not a doctor, but I play one on TV. Did

somebody say deal? A double pleasure is

waiting for you, tra la la la. I liked it so

much I bought the company. Colt 45, works

every time. He loves my mind <u>and</u> he

drinks Johnny Walker. If any of this reminds

you of your portfolio, please get on your

Pontiac and ride. **THE CREATIVE REGISTER.**

Advertising Talent Scouts. (212) 533 3676.

Figure 10.1   A good portfolio should attract job offers, not flies.

10

A Good Book or a Crowbar

Some thoughts on getting into the business

GONE ARE THE DAYS WHEN juniors were hired off the street because of a few promising scribbles on notebook paper and the fire in their eyes. The ad schools are pouring kids out on the street, many of them with highly polished portfolios.

Do you need to go to an ad school?

If you can afford it, if you can put in a couple of years, by all means, go for it.

When I got into the business (without going to an ad school, incidentally), there were only a few such schools in the country. Now they're popping up all over. Regular colleges are also developing ad programs. There is a list of five or six first-rate schools I could include here, but that list may change by the time this book reaches your hands and will likely keep changing. Better to call an agency recruiter or a headhunter and ask who they currently recommend.

If you haven't got the money and can't attend a school, don't give up. The ad programs have no magic bullet. It all comes down to the portfolio of work you put together.

To get a job in the creative side of this business, you will need a portfolio, or what they call a "book." Some 20 to 25 pages of speculative ("spec") ads you've put together to show how you think. If you can put together five or six great campaigns, the top graduate of the best school has nothing on you.

Once you decide to go for it, give it everything. Your portfolio will be the single most important piece you work on in your career. It is your foot in the door, your resume, your agent, spokesperson, and a giant fork in the road in your career. And like a good chess opening, the better it is, the more advantages you will discover through the rest of the game.

Don't worry what kind of portfolio to buy or what it should look like. You'll figure that out later. For now, here's some advice on what to put *in* it.

PUTTING A BOOK TOGETHER

If you're a writer, team up with a promising art director.

If you're an art director, find a writer you get along with. You need each other's skills, and together you may add up to more than the sum of your parts. More than anything, look for someone with energy, with drive. Someone who's hungry. It's a long, uphill battle putting a great book together, so you'll need all the firepower you can muster.

An art director in the mix can help the ads look great. But if you're a writer working alone, you can still pull it off. Remember, creative directors will be looking for the quality of your *ideas.* Handwritten headlines and pencil drawings can serve in a pinch. But with headlines set on somebody's computer, some imaginative use of scrap art or existing photos and a few hours at a copying shop, you can put together a very respectable spec ad.

Here's the big piece of advice. If you remember nothing else, remember this: Spend the time making the concept great, not the execution. John Vitro once told me, "It's not a good idea unless it's a good idea on a plain white sheet of paper."

Here's an example of a concept that's so good, even a bad drawing doesn't get in the way. I am right-handed. With my left hand, I

Figure 10.2   I am right-handed. I have redrawn a famous Nike ad with my left hand to make a point. A highly polished layout of a so-so concept won't hold a candle to a great idea, even one produced like this.

have rendered a famous Nike ad from a British agency (Fig. 10.2). The concept still looks great. Even if your portfolio is a tattered shoe box full of concepts like this, I don't care if they're written in crayon on wet napkins, you will get a job. I guarantee it.

If there's ever a time to study the awards annuals, this is it.

Study them. Read, learn, memorize. Don't just concentrate on the most recent issues, either. Dig up old annuals. Design fads come and go, but the classic advertising structures endure. See what makes the ads work. Take them apart. Put them back together. Some of the ads are humorous and work. Some are straight and work. Why? What's the difference?

For your first portfolio, stick to print.

If you're new to the business, don't try to tackle television or radio. Print's hard enough, and most creative directors I've talked with agree that if you can think conceptually in print, one day you can learn to do the same in broadcast. So stick to print. (Which, in my book, includes outdoor advertising.)

TV boards and radio scripts in a portfolio present themselves so slowly. It's better to have a strong book that presents good print ideas fast, one page after another—whap, whap, whap.

I add this exception: Some ad schools are now equipped with enough video and editing equipment that students can put together rough but respectable TV spots. If you have access to such training and facilities, by all means, take advantage of it. If you don't, do not despair. Print is where you will make your stand.

One way to start is simply to redo some existing ads.

Page through *Time* magazine and look for a bad ad. (You probably won't have to go past page 3.) Find the idea buried in the body copy, where it almost always is. Pull it back out and turn it into an ad.

Round out your portfolio with a variety of goods and services.

If you're just starting out and doing spec ads, don't try to add to the latest, award-winning Nike campaign. It's tempting to do so, but you set yourself up for a harsh comparison to work that's extremely good.

Just pick some products you like. Start a file on them. Fill it with great ads from the awards annuals and bad ads from the magazines. Start jotting down every little thing that feels like an idea. Don't edit. Just start. You like music? Start building a campaign on, say, how this new portable disc player doesn't skip every time you step off the curb. Now find two other products you like. Find what makes them different and do two campaigns there.

Then choose some boring products—products without any differences that distinguish them (besides the ads you're about to do). Insurance. Banking. You figure it out. But find a way to make them interesting.

You might try writing ads for a product you've never used and likely never will. If you're a guy, write subscription ads for *Bride's* magazine. The fresh mind you bring to the category may help your concepts ring new.

And, finally, take a shot at a campaign for a packaged good. Like lipstick, soup, or bullion cubes. But not condoms. Condom ads have been done to death. You won't just be beating a dead horse, you'll be beating the dust from the crumbling rocks of the fossilized bones of a horse crushed between two glaciers in the pre-Cambrian age.

When you're done, your book should show the ability to think creatively and strategically on goods and services, both hard and soft.

One last thing. Avoid public-service campaigns. They're too easy. (*"Hey, look at these fish I caught. Sorry the holes in their heads are so big, but they were in a barrel when I shot them."*)

Now is not the time to play it safe.

As you put your book together, err on the side of recklessness. It's the one time in your career you get to pick the client and write the strategy. If you're not pushing it to the edge now, when are you going to start? It's better to have stuff that's fresh and strategically naive than a nice, sensible portfolio of ads so dull you have to laminate them just to cut down on the smell.

Fill your portfolio with campaigns, not one-shots.

Almost anybody can write a decent headline if they work at it long enough. Only skilled ad people can think in campaigns. Don't send your book out until it has five or six great campaigns in it. And remember, the best campaigns aren't three one-shots strung together by a common typeface, but one big idea executed in a variety of ways. The Absolut vodka or *Rolling Stone* print campaigns shown in Chapter 2 are good examples.

If you have a couple of great one-shots, go ahead, throw 'em in. But they should be icing. Not the cake.

Don't fill your portfolio with cute campaigns for microscopic clients.

A book full of ads for the local bakery, your brother's auto shop, and the dry cleaners will not be very impressive. You need to do ads for checking accounts, newspaper subscriptions, a brand of clothing, a cologne. Real stuff.

These are the tough day-to-day projects you'll actually be working on most of the time in this business. Ads on products like these are a better measure of your abilities than dashing off a zippy headline for portable toilets or an acupuncture parlor.

My friend Bob Barrie has this advice: "Do great ads for boring products."

In addition to having a variety of clients, make sure you show a variety of styles in your book.

Not all headlines, not all visuals, but a good mix of everything you're capable of. This advice applies particularly to aspiring art directors. Show ads that demonstrate your ability to handle type. Ads that are all one visual. Ads with a lot of stuff in them that require good design. Flex a lot of muscles.

If you're looking to land a copywriter's position, have a few samples of copy in your book.

You don't need copy for every ad. Just a few. As your possible creative director, I need to be able to see you know how to write. I need to know that you're comfortable with words, not just ads.

Don't gussy up your portfolio.

Don't spend money on the portfolio case itself or put felt on back of the ads. For one thing, felt backing makes an ad look too important. Come on, it's not the Magna Carta. It's a coupon ad for Jell-O. Felt also takes up too much room, and I can make my portfolio beat your portfolio with more great work in the same amount of space. Laminate if you want, but if you can't afford it, don't worry about it. I refer you again to my left-handed drawing of that famous Nike ad. Forget the packaging. The work is everything.

Don't do "clever" mailers.

It's tempting to demonstrate your creativity this way. But don't. I've seen the weirdest things sent to the agency. A foot from a department store dummy in a box topped with the expected line: "I'd love to get my foot in the door of your agency." I've seen about 20 of those. One guy tiptoed into the mail room and sat inside a Federal Express box. The *creepiest* one was an envelope stuffed with "bloody" bandages with some message about how "I'd kill to work at your agency."

Don't do it. I've never seen anything as clever as a good portfolio.

Don't do a cute resume.

Your portfolio is where you should showcase your creativity. Your resume should say who you are. Keep it to one page and get right to the point. This is my name. I'm a writer or I'm an art director. This is the job I want. Here's my experience, my address, and my phone number. Thank you and good night.

If you're just beginning, don't count on a headhunter to find you a job.

Typically, headhunters work with midlevel to senior positions that have higher salary potential. (They make their money on a percentage of the salary.) Most agencies aren't interested in paying recruiters' fees to fill entry-level jobs when they're getting all the applicants they can handle walking in off the street.

"Networking."

I swore I'd never use the word as a verb, but nothing else seems to fit here. If you don't have relatives working in the business, networking's precisely the thing you'll have to do. You'll have to send out feelers far and wide.

Tell every living person you know you're trying to land a job at an ad agency. You may find that the friend of a friend has a name. And a name is all you need to start building your contacts.

So you ask around and get a name. Maybe he or she doesn't even work in the creative department. It doesn't matter—you call. Even if they're not hiring, you ask for an "information interview" or advice on your book.

When you meet this person, be your usual charming self. Don't be too flip, go through the mail on his desk, or make funny comments about the pictures of his kids. Just listen. Then politely ask if he knows of job openings anywhere. Get the name of another contact. Ask if you can use his name to get in the door somewhere *else*. Keep this up and over time you'll slowly fatten your Rolodex with names, numbers, and contacts. One day the phone will ring.

I was lucky. In my case, it went like this—my college roommate's wife's brother was the president of a local agency, Bozell & Jacobs. So I called my old buddy. He talked to his wife. She talked to her brother. And he said to have me call this guy in his creative department—some guy named Tom McElligott.

Establish a phone or mail relationship with a working writer or art director.

There are plenty of friendly and helpful people in the business who will be willing to help you along. The trick is finding one.

Take a risk. Write a letter to somebody whose work you admire. Tell him that. No brownnosing. Just matter-of-factly tell him you're trying to get into the business and ask if he could take a look at your work and give you advice on how to improve it.

Once you get a dialogue going, there are two important things to do: (1) Give serious consideration to the advice you get, and (2) don't stalk him. Keep a respectful distance. Don't call more than once or twice. Send a thank-you note. And get back to him only when you have significantly improved your book.

—————

THE INTERVIEW

Before each interview, study the agency.

It's probably smart to begin your search by looking closely at the agencies that are doing work compatible with your style.

Read the latest awards books and familiarize yourself with their best work. Memorize the names of their top clients. Learn the names of the people who created their best work and check to make sure they still work there.

You'll find client lists, billings, and other stuff in a big fat book called *The Standard Directory of Advertising Agencies,* known in the business as the "Red Book." There's a similar sourcebook, *Adweek's Agency Directory,* available through the magazine. If neither book is available at your local library, borrow one from a friendly agency, xerox the places you want to hit, and study them.

Of course, none of this is for the purposes of brownnosing. *("Gee, Mr. Hanson, I thought your work for Spray 'n' Wipe was so meaningful.")* What it says is that you're a student of the business and you're serious enough about getting into it that you've done your homework.

Take care that the agency you select isn't doing good work on only one account.

If that's the case, it may say more about how good the client is than the agency. Once you get on board, you may find that the bulk of the clients, the ones that pay the bills, aren't producing decent work. The really good agencies do good work for most or all of their accounts.

If you can't get in to the see the general, talk to a lieutenant.

You don't have to get an interview with the creative director to get your foot in the door at an agency. If you have a great book, see if you can get 15 minutes of time with a senior creative person. They know when the agency is hiring, even if they're not the ones doing it. If they like you, it's relatively easy for them to slide your portfolio under the CD's nose at the right moment.

If you come on board and do great work, it reflects well on them. I've helped several juniors get on board and have watched with some measure of undeserved pride when a kid "I discovered" does well.

It may happen for you this way. If it does, maybe you can return the favor someday to a kid who comes into your office with a bad haircut and a great book. Take the time to help him. We're all in this together.

In the interview, don't just sit there.

I don't care how good your book is, you can't just throw it on a CD's desk, park yourself on his sofa, and wait to discuss company health

plans and vacation time. You must make it clear you have a pulse.
Advertising is a business that requires a lot of people skills, and it
will help if your CD sees you have them—that you're personable,
that you can handle a business meeting with verve and confidence,
and generally aren't a stick-in-the mud.

Trust your instincts.

Go to ten different interviews and you're going to get ten different
opinions on your work. It will be confusing. *("The guy with the sus-*
penders liked this campaign, but the guy with the ponytail said it
sucked.")

If the majority say the same thing, take the hint. But you don't
have to agree with everybody. If you do, you'll water down your
book. Trust your instincts. Keep what you believe in. Change what
you don't. Keep reworking your book until the weak parts are out
and the good parts are great.

One way to get a good read on what needs improving is to ask
each person you meet in an interview what he thinks is the weakest
campaign in your book. If more than a couple point to the same
campaign, take it around the back of the barn. You know what to do.

Have an opinion.

This is another version of "Trust your instincts."

If the interviewer asks you what kind of advertising you like or
what campaigns you wish you had done (and many do), don't be
afraid to have an opinion. Say what current or classic campaigns you
like and describe why. It's a subjective business, and unless you pick
Mr. Whipple as your dream campaign, you'll probably do fine.

What's bad is having no opinion at all. "Oh, I like . . . well, I like
whatever's good is what I like."

Offer to do the grunt work.

My very first assignment in the business was to write some 50 "live"
radio scripts for a hotel corporation. Live radio is simply a script
read by the local DJ in between the farm and wrestling reports. I sus-

pect if that awful live radio job hadn't come through the agency door, I might not have either. But I was more than happy to do it.

I recommend you take the same attitude. Express your willingness to take on any assignment they throw at you. Many young people come in wanting to work on an agency's national TV accounts. While it's possible, it's more likely you'll have to pay your dues first. Get ready to do some live radio, or what we cynics call "the brochures of the airwaves."

Have a small version of your portfolio ready to leave behind after the interview.

They may not have room for you today. But it's my experience that agencies keep files on promising creatives. So have a good-looking, nicely bound 8½- by 11-inch version of your book ready to leave behind. Color copies are nice but aren't absolutely necessary. Great work communicates in black and white, too.

Save your big interviews for last.

Use the early interviews for practice, first hitting those agencies that are farther down on your preference list.

Interviews can seem kind of scary at first. But if you can get a few under your belt successfully, get some experience fielding questions and showing work, you'll increase your confidence. Confidence that will show when you finally interview at those special agencies where you really want to land a job.

If you can't get into the creative department, get into the agency.

I can name quite a few good creative people who started their agency careers in the mail room, or as coordinators, secretaries, even account executives. Ed McCabe, for example—mail-room boy.

The thing is, once you're in, you can learn more. You'll be able to watch it happen firsthand. You'll also start making friends with people who can hire you or help move you into the creative department. Unlike companies such as IBM, ad agencies are loosely structured places that often fill job openings with any knucklehead who proves he can do the work. They don't care what you majored in.

So get in there, do the job, keep your ears open, your book fresh, and when a creative position opens up, who do you think they'll hire? A stranger off the street or the smart young kid in the mail room who's paid his dues and is still chomping at the bit.

How to talk about money.

I had a long discussion about money matters with Dany Lennon, one of the best creative recruiters in the ad business. (The ad that opens this chapter, for "The Creative Register," that's her recruitment agency.) She gave me this advice and I pass it on to you.

"Do your homework," Dany told me. "Before you go into an interview you should know what the starting salary levels for that city, and that area, are. Talk to headhunters, talk to the agency recruiters, make phone calls, but find out. Then, when you and the creative director begin to talk about money, you won't be left in the position of saying, 'Okay, so what do *you* think I'm worth?' An agency might be tempted to lowball you.

"Instead you say, 'Well, this is what I understand to be the starting salary at comparable agencies in this area.' Drop the name of an agency if you like. But take the *responsibility* of knowing about money. Don't leave it up to the agency. If you do it forthrightly, your CD is going to see an intelligent person who's done their homework, and money won't be a federal case. Just one of fairness. It's not so much the money you get that matters anyway, but the *way* in which you conduct yourself during the negotiation. A mature, intelligent, and fair negotiation says a lot about your character, also very important in an interview.

"Once you've negotiated your salary," Dany went on, "you may want to tell your CD you would appreciate a review in six months. Not a raise, but a review. This says to him, 'I'm going to work my tail off for this place and I'm confident in six months you'll see you've made a great hire.' And six months is all it usually takes for a CD to get a good read on you: on how hard you work, your attitude, your overall value to his company."

More than anything, Dany warned me, don't cop an attitude and start pitting one agency's offer against another. According to Lennon, there is, unfortunately, a burgeoning "brat pack" movement within the industry. Standard starting salaries, which were once etched in stone, are a thing of the past and negotiations are more common. Not a bad thing in itself, but it has created a situation where talented newcomers are swaggering into agencies with good portfolios and bad attitudes.

I heard this story from the president of one of the country's top ad schools. He happens to be visiting a New York agency, chatting in the office of the creative director. Phone rings and it's a young graduate of another ad school. (The agency had previously agreed to fly this kid up to New York for a better look at him and his book—translation: a real interview and a likely job offer.)

But on the phone, the kid "cops a 'tude" and tells the agency CD he isn't coming unless he makes such-and-such kind of money (a salary *way* outside of what juniors usually make). Before slam-welding the phone receiver to its cradle, the creative director shrieks into it a string of invectives so toxic that common decency prevents their retelling here.

A man named Frederick Collins once said, "There are two types of people in the world. Those who come into a room and say, 'Well, here I am!' and those who come in and say, 'Ah, there you are.' "

Be that second type of person.

Don't choose an agency based on the salary they offer.

If you're lucky enough to get a couple of offers, you may find that the better salary is offered by the worse agency. It has always been thus. And Lord knows, it will be tempting to take that extra money when it's held out to you. Don't.

One of Bill Bernbach's best lines was, "It isn't a principle until it costs you money." In this case, the principle in question is the value you place on doing great work. I urge you to go with the agency that's producing good advertising. You may work for less, but it's more likely you'll produce better ads. And in the long run, nothing is better for a great salary than a great book.

More than once I've seen a talented kid go for the bigger check at a bad agency and a year later take a cut in pay just to get the hell out of there. The bad part was that even after a year in the belly of the beast, he hadn't added so much as a brochure to his original student portfolio.

If you get a fair offer from a good agency, take it. Take in four roommates if you have to, live in your parents' basement, but get on board—that's the trick. I read somewhere not to set your sights on money anyway. Just do what you do well and the money will come. McElligott once told me "You'll be underpaid the first half of your career and overpaid the second."

Take a job wherever you can and work hard.

All you need to do to get on a roll is to produce a couple of great campaigns and have them run. And it's possible to do great work at almost any agency in America. (Note judicious use of the word "possible.") Once you do a great campaign, once it gets in the books, creative directors everywhere will see your name. And you can make the next move up.

Don't be crestfallen if you can't get into one of the "hot" shops. The agency offering you the job can be a stepping-stone. (It's probably not a good idea to tell them this as you're shaking hands: "Thank you, sir. I guess this will just have to do until something opens up at Wieden & Kennedy. In fact, I think I'll just leave my coat on if you don't mind.")

Remember, wherever you land a job, there'll be plenty to learn from the people you'll meet. Think of that first job as continuing your education.

Just get on board and work like hell. Early in your career's the time to do it, too, when you don't have children calling you on the phone asking how to get the top off the gasoline can in the garage.

It may seem that you can't outthink those senior creatives right now, but you can definitely outwork them. Make hard work your secret weapon.

SOME FINAL THOUGHTS

Once you land a job, stick with it awhile.

There are going to be rough spots no matter where you work. There are no perfect agencies. I like to think I have worked at a couple of the best, and there were plenty of times I thought just about everything that could be wrong was wrong.

Hang in there for awhile. Things can change. An account that's miserable one year can suddenly become the one everybody wants to work on. There's also value in learning to stick with something long enough to see it through.

If you've heard that the best way to increase your salary is to change jobs, it's true. But I advise against job-hopping solely for that reason. If you're at a good agency making a fair wage, stay there. Every six months or so, take a long hard look at your portfolio. If it's getting better, stay. Move on only when you've learned as much as you possibly can. You don't want a resume that's a long list of brief stints at agency after agency.

Don't let advertising mess up your life.

On the same page that I say work hard, I also warn against working to the exclusion of all else. We all seem to take this silly advertising stuff so seriously.

Some of us end up working way too hard and ignoring our spouses, our partners, our friends, and our lives. Remember, ultimately, it's just advertising. Compared to the important things in life, even a commercial that runs on the Super Bowl is still just an overblown coupon ad for Jell-O. Love, happiness, stability, sanity, *those* are the important things. Don't forget it.

Don't underestimate yourself.

Don't think, "I shouldn't bother sending my book to that agency. They're too good."

All people are subject to low self-esteem and I think creative people are particularly prone to it. I can think of several people in our creative department who didn't think they were good enough, but sent their book on a lark and we took them up on it.

Don't overestimate yourself.

For some reason, a lot of people in this business develop huge egos. Yet none of us is saving lives. We are glorified sign painters and nothing more.

Get paid to think up stuff like this.

Some ad agency actually paid a writer and an art director to think up this crazy visual idea for an ad. But coming up with wildly creative solutions to real marketing problems is what advertising is all about. And, after 8 semesters at Art Center, you'll have a good portfolio and a good shot at landing a job in a field that's financially **ArtCenter** as well as creatively rewarding. Call us at 818-584-5035. Or write to Admissions, Art Center College of Design, 1700 Lida St., Pasadena, CA, 91103.

Figure 11.1   Although Joe Paprocki and I did this ad, we didn't think up the visual for it. We just borrowed it from some other ad. Then we went to lunch. What a great business.

11

Making Shoes versus Making Shoe Commercials

Is this a great business or what?

WHAT MAKES THIS BUSINESS GREAT ARE all the knuckleheads. All the people just slightly left of center. This business seems to attract them.

People who don't find fulfillment anywhere in the business world somehow end up on advertising's doorstep, their personal problems clanking behind like cans in back of a just-married car. They come for personal reasons, with their own agendas. They bring to the business creativity, energy, and chaos and from the business they get discipline, perspective, and maturity.

All in all, they make for an interesting day at the office, these oddballs, artists, misfits, cartoonists, poets, beatniks, creepy quiet guys, and knuckleheads. What's even better—they all seem to have a wonderful sense of humor. It's just one comedian after another all the way down the hallway. Knuckleheads in the mail room, knuckleheads answering the phones, they're in the CEO's office, they're everywhere.

———

I'm on a morning flight to a client meeting in St. Louis. It's just me and my old boss, the president of a large advertising agency.

It's not a full flight, so I stake a claim to an empty row, set up shop, and get a little work done. My boss settles down a row behind me. After awhile, I doze off. When I wake up 20 minutes later, my tray table is down and on it, wide open to the centerfold, is a *Penthouse* magazine.

Behind me I can hear my boss, snickering.

God only knows how many *stewardesses* have walked by, seen me slumped there, my mouth gaping open. Twitching, probably.

Thinking back now, it pleases me that a big, important ad executive like my boss could take the time, even during his busy day, to abuse and degrade one lowly employee like me.

———

This is a great business.

Look at what you're doing. You're an image merchant. You're weaving words and pictures together and imbuing inanimate objects with meaning and value.

Mark Fenske said advertising is the world's most powerful art form. Is he right? Well, Picasso was great, but I've never looked at one of his paintings and then walked off and did something Pablo wanted me to. Advertising, like no other form of creative communication, has the power to affect what people do.

It works.

In the 20s, Claude Hopkins sat down in his office at Lord & Thomas and wrote "Drink an orange." A nation began drinking fruit juice.

Steve Hayden sat down in his office at Chiat/Day and wrote "Why 1984 won't be like 1984" for Apple computers. A nation began thinking maybe computers belong in living rooms, not just in corporations.

Dan Wieden sat down, wrote "Just Do It," and changed the world. In 1978, there weren't many joggers on the side of the road. (Even the *word* didn't exist. "Jogging." What the hell was that?) Now you can't throw a stick out the window without hitting five of them.

"Nike killed the three-martini lunch," says Fenske. Nike told us to get off our collective butt and just do it and suddenly it wasn't okay anymore to lie around on the couch wallpapering our arteries with lard. We started taking the stairs. At the wheel of this national change of heart: an advertiser, a great agency, and the world's most powerful art form—advertising.

Whether you agree with Fenske that "Nike and Coke brought down the Berlin Wall," the power of advertising to globalize icons and homogenize the buying habits of whole continents is undeniable.

In *Adcult USA,* James Twitchell wrote:

[Advertising] has collapsed . . . cultures into a monolithic, worldwide order immediately recognized by the House of Windsor and the tribe of Zulu. . . . If ever there is to be a global village, it will be because the town crier works in advertising.[1]

———

This is a great business.

Look at what you're getting paid for—putting your feet up and thinking. This is what people with real jobs do when they get time *off*—put their feet up and daydream, drift, and think of goofy stuff. You, you're getting a paycheck for it.

I remember we had this new secretary in the creative department. He kept walking into the offices of art directors and writers, interrupting their work, just to chat. Somebody finally said to him: "Listen, we'd like to talk, but we've gotta get this done, so if you could . . ."

He backed out of the room, apologizing: "Jeez, I'm sorry. You had your feet up, you were talking, laughing. It didn't look like you were working."

———

This is, indeed, a great business.

This fact was recently brought home to me during a train ride from downtown Chicago to O'Hare airport.

I'd just left a very bad meeting where a client had killed a whole bunch of my work. I fumed for the first couple of miles. (*"Those were great ads! They can't kill those ads!"*)

As I sat there feeling sorry for myself, the gray factories passed by the train window. Miles of factories. On the loading docks, I could see hundreds of hardworking people. Laborers forklifting crates of Bic pens onto trucks, hauling boxes of canned peaches onto freight cars. They'd been there since 6:00 in the morning, maybe 5:00. These were hardworking people. With real jobs.

And then there was me, feeling sorry for myself as I whipped by in an air-conditioned train on the way to my happy little seat on the plane with its free peanuts. Peanuts roasted and packed by some worker in another gray factory as he looked up at the clock on the high brick wall, waiting for the minute hand to hit that magic 10:30 mark so he could get out of the noise for 15 minutes, drink a Coke, smoke a Winston, and then it's back to my stinkin' peanuts.

I must remember this.

There are research firms out there that will tell me the sky isn't blue. Clients that will kill an ad because it has a flyswatter in it. And agencies that will make fortunes on ideas like Mr. Whipple. Yet, tomorrow, I'll be back in the hallways telling jokes with the funniest people in corporate America, putting my feet up on marble table-tops, and getting paid to think. Nothing more. Just to think. And talk about movies.

You should remember this, too.

You'll be paid a lot of money in this business. You'll never have to do any heavy lifting. Never have dirt under your fingernails or an aching back when you come home from work. You're *lucky* to be talented. *Lucky* to get into the business.

Stay humble.

SUGGESTED READING

Read every old One Show and *Communication Arts* you can get your hands on. Read every British *Design & Art Direction* annual you can find. Become a student of advertising history.

On the subject of history, I'll also mention *When Advertising Tried Harder,* by Larry Dubrow; *Remember Those Great Volkswagen Ads?* by David Abbott; and *From Those Wonderful Folks Who Brought You Pearl Harbor,* by Jerry Della Femina.

Adcult USA: The Triumph of Advertising in American Culture. James B. Twitchell's exploration of the profound influence of advertising on American culture is remarkable.

Advertising: Concept and Copy, by George Felton, is a wonderful textbook on the craft. Excellent, detailed advice on how to think, how to write. Good stuff.

How to Succeed in Advertising When All You Have Is Talent, by Minksy and Calvo, is a great collection of thoughtful interviews with some of the biggest names in the business.

Positioning by Reis and Trout. Although I'm not very impressed by any of the ads they use as examples, they are good strategic thinkers.

Strunk & White's *Elements of Style* is required reading for anyone who holds a pencil anywhere near paper.

"I Can See you Naked": A Fearless Guide to Making Great Presentations, by Ron Hoff. A great book on getting rid of the butterflies and putting on good presentations.

For the sheer joy of writing I recommend Natalie Goldberg's *Writing Down the Bones* and Ann Lamott's *Bird by Bird.*

If you're just trying to break into the business, I recommend Maxine Paetro's book, *How to Put Your Book Together and Get a Job in Advertising.*

And, if you can get them to, have your *client* read Dick Wasserman's wonderful book, *That's Our New Ad Campaign?*

For those interested in further study, one of the best bibliographies I've found is in *Advertising in America: The First 200 Years* by Goodrum and Dalrymple.

BIBLIOGRAPHY

Adams, James, L. *Conceptual Blockbusting.* Reading, MA: Addison-Wesley Publishing Co. Inc., 1974.

Bernbach, Bill. *Bill Bernbach said . . .* New York: DDB Needham, 1995.

Burton, Phillip Ward, and Scott C. Purvis. *Which Ad Pulled Best: 50 Case Histories on How to Write and Design Ads That Work.* Lincolnwood, IL: NTC Business Books, 1996.

Clark, Eric. *The Want Makers.* New York: Viking, 1988.

Cook, Marshall. *Freeing Your Creativity: A Writer's Guide.* Cincinnati, OH: Writer's Digest Books, 1992.

Corporate Report magazine, Minneapolis, MN, 1982.

D&AD Mastercraft Series. *The Copy Book.* Switzerland: Rotovision, 1995.

D&AD Mastercraft Series. *The Art Director Book.* Switzerland: Rotovision, 1997.

Foster, Jack. *How to Get Ideas.* San Francisco: Berret-Koehler Publishers, 1996.

Goodrum, Charles, and Helen Dalrymple. *Advertising in America: The First 200 Years.* New York: Harry N. Abrams, Incorporated, 1990.

Gossage, Howard Luck. *The Book of Gossage.* Chicago: The Copy Workshop, 1995.

Higgins, Denis. *The Art of Writing Advertising.* Lincolnwood, IL: NTC Business Books, 1965.

Hoff, Ron. *I Can See You Naked.* Kansas City, MO: Andrews & McMeel, 1992.

Ind, Nicholas. *Great Advertising Campaigns.* Lincolnwood, IL: NTC Business Books, 1993.

Lamott, Anne. *Bird by Bird.* New York: Doubleday, 1994.

Lyons, John. *Guts. Advertising from the Inside Out.* New York: Amacom, 1987.

Matthews, John E. *The Copywriter.* Glen Ellyn, IL: self-published, 1964.

Mayer, Martin. *Whatever Happened to Madison Avenue?* Boston, MA: Little Brown & Company, 1991.

McAlhone, Beryl, and David Stuart. *A Smile in the Mind: Witty Thinking in Graphic Design.* London: Phaidon Press Ltd., 1996.

Monahan, Tom. From *Communication Arts* magazine, Palo Alto, CA.

Ogilvy, David. *Confessions of an Advertising Man.* New York: Atheneum, 1963.

One Club, The. *Pencil Pointers* newsletter. New York, 1995.

Paetro, Maxine. *How to Put Your Book Together and Get a Job in Advertising.* Chicago, IL: The Copy Workshop, 1990.

Reis, Al, and Jack Trout. *Marketing Warfare.* New York: McGraw-Hill, 1986.

Reis, Al, and Jack Trout. *Positioning: The Battle for Your Mind.* New York: McGraw-Hill, 1981.

Roman, Kenneth, and Jane Maas. *The New How to Advertise.* New York: St. Martin's Press, 1992.

Schulberg, Bob. *Radio Advertising: The Authoritative Handbook.* Lincolnwood, IL: NTC Business Books, 1994.

Wakeman, Fred. *The Hucksters.* Scranton, PA: Rinehart & Company, 1946.

Wallace, Dave. *Break Out!* Grand Rapids, MI: Ainsco Incorporated, 1994.

Wall Street Journal, Creative Leaders Series. New York: Dow Jones & Company, 1993.

Wasserman, Dick. *That's Our New Ad Campaign?* New York: The New Lexington Press, 1988.

Weiner, Ellis. *Decade of the Year,* New York: Dutton, 1982.

Young, James Webb. *Technique for Producing Ideas.* Chicago, IL: Advertising Publications, Inc., 1944.

ACKNOWLEDGMENTS

Cover design by WORK, Richmond, Virginia. Art director/designer: Tom Gibson

I would like to thank the following people for help in writing this book: My wife, Curlin Reed Sullivan, Bob Barrie, Jamie Barrett, Betsy Barnum, Andre Bergeron, Kevin Berigan, Bob Blewett, Laurie Brown, Rob Buchner, Pat Burnham, Scott Cooley, Russel Curtis, Gina Dante, Pat Fallon, Mark Fenske, Kevin Flatt, Anne Fredrickson, Tom Gibson, Wayne Gibson, Glenn Gill, Al Hampel, Phil Hanft, Cabell Harris, David Jelly Helm, Carol Henderson, Joel Herrmann, Bill Hillsman, Adrian Hilton, Sally Hogshead, Mike Hughes, Gary Johns, Kathy Jydstrup, Lori Kraft, Jim Lacey, Greg Lane, Dany Lennon, Andy Lerner, Mike Lescarbeau, Tom Lichtenheld, John Mahoney, Tom McElligott, Tom McEnery, Doug Melroe, Karen Melvin, Lucy Meredith, Ruth Mills, Larry Minsky, Tom Monahan, Ty Montague, Ken Musto, Tom Nelson, Diane O'Hara, Kevin Proudfoot, Kathy Orman, Col. William Preston Reed, Joey Reiman, Mike Renfro, Tom Rosen, Nancy Rubenstein, Stacy Runkel, Daniel Russ,

Ron Seichrist, Fred, Marty, and Jennifer Senn, Mal Sharpe, Joan Shealy, Montrew Smith, Pete Smith, Thad Spencer, Myra Longstreet Sullivan, Joe Sweet, Kirsten Taklo, Diane Cook Tench, Mary Tetlow, Tom Thomas, Jerry Torchia, Eric Valentine, Rob Van, Carol Vick, Christa von staaveren, Craig Weise, Howard Willenzik, Judy Wittenberg, and Steve Wolff.

NOTES

CHAPTER ONE

1. Mayer, *Whatever Happened to Madison Avenue?,* p. 46.
2. Roman and Maas, *The New How to Advertise,* p. 38.
3. Lyons, *Guts,* p. 115.
4. Wakeman, Fred. *The Hucksters.* Scranton, PA: Rinehart & Company, 1946, p. 22.
5. Ibid., p. 45.
6. *Wall Street Journal, Creative Leaders Series,* p. 12.
7. Bernbach, *Bill Bernbach said . . .* Not paginated.
8. Souder, William. "Hot Shop." *Corporate Report* (September 1982).
9. Ward, John, "Four Facets of Advertising Performance Measurement." In Chris Baker, ed., *The Longer and Broader Effects of Advertising.* London: Institute of Practitioners in Advertising, 1990, p. 44.
10. Karl, Sandra. "Creative Man Helmut Krone Talks About the Making of an Ad." *Advertising Age* (October 14, 1968).
11. Bernbach, *Bill Bernbach said . . .* Not paginated.

CHAPTER TWO

1. Charlton, James, ed. *The Writer's Quotation Book, A Literary Companion*. New York: Viking-Penguin, 1980, p. 55.
2. *Wall Street Journal* "Creative Leaders Series," p. 5.
3. Fallon McElligott agency research.
4. Clark, *The Want Makers*, p. 24.
5. Young, James Webb. *Technique for Producing Ideas*. Chicago, IL: Advertising Publications, Inc., 1944.
6. D&AD Mastercraft Series. *The Copy Book*, p. 68.
7. *Wall Street Journal* "Creative Leaders Series," p. 12.

CHAPTER THREE

1. Fallon, Pat. "Why Pit Positioning Against Creativity?" *Advertising Age* (August 7, 1989).
2. Clark, *The Want Makers*, p. 54
3. Reis and Trout, *Marketing Warfare*, p. 70.
4. Lamott, *Bird by Bird*, 1994, p. 23.
5. Cook, Marshall. *Freeing Your Creativity: A Writer's Guide*. Cincinnati, OH: Writer's Digest Books, 1992, p. 7.
6. D&AD Mastercraft Series. *The Art Director Book*, p. 44.
7. Bernbach, *Bill Bernbach said . . .* Not paginated.
8. Adams, *Conceptual Blockbusting*, p. 66.
9. McAlhone and Stuart, *A Smile in the Mind: Witty Thinking in Graphic Design*, p. 19.
10. Wallace, *Break Out!*, p. 41.
11. Felton, George. *Advertising: Concept and Copy*. Englewood Cliffs, New Jersey: Prentice Hall, 1994, p. 80.

CHAPTER FOUR

1. Charlton, *The Writer's Quotation Book, A Literary Companion*, p. 44.
2. Gossage, Howard Luck. *The Book of Gossage*. Chicago: The Copy Workshop, 1995, pp. 114, 115.
3. Burton, Phillip Ward, and Scott C. Purvis. *Which Ad Pulled Best: 50 Case Histories on How to Write and Design Ads That Work*. Lincolnwood, IL: NTC Business Books, 1996, p. 24.

4. Karl. "Creative Man Helmut Krone Talks About the Making of an Ad."
5. Lyons, *Guts,* p. 167.
6. Kneller, George. *The Art and Science of Creativity.* New York: Holt, Rinehart & Winston, 1965, p. 55.
7. *Wall Street Journal* "Creative Leaders Series," p. 20.

CHAPTER SIX

1. Monahan, *Communication Arts,* July 1994, p. 198.

CHAPTER SEVEN

1. Karl. "Creative Man Helmut Krone Talks About the Making of an Ad."
2. A sidenote on one of the most misquoted lines in our industry: "pushing the envelope." The correct version, "pushing the outside of the envelope," was first popularized by Tom Wolfe's wonderful book *The Right Stuff.* Test pilots, before flying a newly designed airplane, were sometimes handed envelopes containing the specifications of the aircraft and its performance limitations. During a test flight, the pilots would then push the aircraft to its limit, to the edge of its capabilities— thus, "pushing the outside of the envelope." On the other hand, "pushing the envelope," as it is often misquoted by agency people, means nothing more than the "movement of stationery." As in: "My boss grew so tired of my misuse of Tom Wolfe's phrase that he pushed the envelope containing my severance pay across his desk and said 'You're fired.'"
3. Pope, Daniel. *The Making of Modern Advertising.* New York: Basic Books, 1983, p. 4.

CHAPTER EIGHT

1. *Wall Street Journal* "Creative Leaders Series," p. 44.
2. Weiner, Ellis. *Decade of the Year,* New York: Dutton, 1982.

CHAPTER NINE

1. Hoff, *I Can See You Naked,* p. 30.
2. Ibid.

3. Wasserman, *That's Our New Ad Campaign?*, p. 3.

4. Crompton, Alastair, *The Craft of Copywriting, How to Write Great Copy That Sells.* Englewood Cliffs, New Jersey: Prentice-Hall, Inc., 1979, p. 166.

5. *Wall Street Journal* "Creative Leaders Series," p. 20.

6. Monahan, *Communication Arts,* May/June 1994, p. 29.

7. Schulberg, Bob. *Radio Advertising: The Authoritative Handbook.* Lincolnwood, IL: NTC Business Books, 1994, p. 234.

8. Delaney, Tim. "Basic Instincts." *One to One: Newsletter of One Club for Art & Copy,* November/December 1994, p. 1.

9. Monahan, *Communication Arts,* September/October 1994, p. 67.

10. Wasserman, *That's Our New Ad Campaign?*, pp. 37, 38.

11. Bernbach, *Bill Bernbach said . . .* Not paginated.

12. Jeweler, Dr. A. Jerome. *Creative Strategies in Advertising.* Belmont, CA. Wadsworth-ITP Publishing, 1995, p. 171.

CHAPTER ELEVEN

1. Twitchell, James B. *Adcult USA: The Triumph of Advertising in American Culture.* New York: Columbia University, 1996, p. 43.

AD CREDITS

Fig. 1.2: Volkswagen "Lemon"—CW: Julian Koenig, AD: Helmut Krone; Fig. 2.1: Crispin & Porter—CW: Chuck Porter, AD: Alex Bogusky; Fig. 2.2: Penn—CW: Mike Gibbs, AD: John Seymour-Anderson; Fig. 2.3: Absolut— CD: Arnie Arlow, CW: Alix Botwin, AD: David Oakley; Copy on left side of ad: Lou Graham, from *The Seventh Sister,* copyright 1985; Fig. 2.4: *Rolling Stone:* CW: Bill Miller, AD: Nancy Rice; Fig. 3.1: Dublin Advertising Photography—CW: Mike Lescarbeau, AD: Bob Barrie; Fig. 3.2: American Floral Marketing Council—CW: Dean Buckhorn, AD: Barbara Scardino; Fig. 3.3: *Family Life* magazine—CW: Luke Sullivan, AD: Joe Paprocki; Fig. 3.4: Volkswagen "It makes your house look bigger."—CW: Bob Levenson, AD: Len Sirowitz; Fig. 3.5: Taronga Zoo—CW/AD: George Betsis & Siimon Reynolds; Fig. 3.6: PETA—CW: Luke Sullivan, AD: Wayne Gibson; Fig. 3.7: 1879 Diebold Safe & Lock Company, from *Advertising in America: The First 200 Years* by Charles Goodrum and Helen Dalrymple; Fig. 3.8: Mitsubishi—CW: Antony Redman, AD: Andy Clarke; Fig. 3.9: Fisher-Price— CW: Frank Budgen, AD: Bill Gallacher; Fig. 3.10: *The Economist* keyhole—CW: Richard Foster, AD: John Horton; Fig. 3.11: Barnett Banks: CW: Luke Sullivan, AD: Diane Cook-Tench; Fig. 3.12: *The Economist* message on top of bus—CW: Malcolm Duffy, David Abbott, AD: Paul Briginshaw; Fig. 3.13: Nike—Phil Cockrell, AD: Graham Storey; Fig. 3.14: Volvo—CW: Minoru Kawase, AD: Masakazu Sawa; Fig. 3.15: 1915 U.S. Army recruitment poster from Hoover Institutional Archives, Stanford University—Artist: Fred Spear; Fig. 3.16: Pan Am Airlines: CW & AD: unknown; Fig. 3.17: drawn by Tom Lichtenheld; Fig. 3.18: Lee Jeans—CW: Luke Sullivan, AD: Arty Tan; Fig. 4.1: Volkswagen—CW: John Withers, AD: Helmut Krone (with apologies to Mr. Krone for reformatting type to improve legibility); Fig. 4.2: Volkswagen—CW: Tony Cox, AD: Mark Reddy; Fig. 4.3: Four Corners—CW: Paul Marshall, AD: Gary Marshall; Fig. 4.4: NYNEX Yellow Pages—CW: Dion Hughes, AD: Cabell Harris; Fig. 4.5: Avis—CW: Paula Green; AD: Helmut Krone; Fig. 5.1: Oregon Film Board—CW: Glen Cole, AD: John Boiler; Fig. 5.2: Apple Computers: CW: Steve Hayden, AD: Brent Thomas, Lee Clow; Fig. 5.3: Maxell—CW: Peter Levathes; AD: Lars Anderson; Fig. 5.4: FMC—CW: John Mahoney, AD: Hal Tench; Fig. 5.5: Honda—CW: Bob Coburn, AD: Gary Yoshida, TALENT IN SPOT: Albie Selznick, represented by Susan Nathe & Assoc., LA; Fig. 5.6: Penn—CW: Jarl Olsen, AD: Houman Pirdavari; Fig. 5.7: Snapple—CW: Risa Mickenberg, AD: Amy Nicholson; Fig. 5.8: Federal Express—CW: Patrick Kelly, AD: Michael Tesch; Fig. 5.9: Nike—CW: Bob Moore, AD: Warren Eakins; Fig. 5.10: Alaska Airlines—CW: Jim Copacino, AD: Jerry Box; Fig. 5.11: Wendy's—CW: Cliff Freeman; AD: Donna Weinheim, Jean Govoni; Fig. 6.1: Radio In The Nude—CW: Doug de Grood, AD: Bob Brihn; Radio commercials: First Tennessee—CWs: Pat Burnham and Phil Hanft; Duracell Batteries—CW: David McGrath; Valley Olds-Pontiac-GMC—CW: Craig Weise; *Crain's New York*—CW: Dean Hacohen; Tuffy's dog food—CW: John Jarvis; Phillips—CW: Tim Delaney, Griff Rhys Jones, Mel Smith; American Spirit Insurance—CW: Mike Renfro; Ortho Ant-Stop Fire Ant Killer—CW: April Winchel; Washington Apples—CW: John Crawford & Ian Hadley; Fig. 7.1: Nike—CW: Jamie Barrett, AD: David Jelly Helm; Fig. 7.2: Nike—CW: Jamie Barrett, AD: David Jelly Helm; Fig. 8.1: AD2—CW: Jo Marshall, AD: Ann Riebe-Rhodes; Fig. 8.2. International Paper—CW: Billings Fuess, AD: Belinda Lee/Alistair Proctor/Herb Jager; Fig. 9.1: Asche & Spencer Music—CW: Luke Sullivan, AD: Bob Barrie; Fig. 9.4: Little Caesar's—CW: Cliff Freeman, AD: Donna Weinheim; Fig. 10.1: The Creative Register—CW: Ty Montague, AD: Nick Cohen; Fig. 10.2: Nike—CW: Tim Riley, AD: Andy McKay; Fig. 11.1: Art Center—CW: Luke Sullivan, AD: Joe Paprocki. **NOTE: More of my own ads than I originally intended appear in this book. Many ads that would have served better were either unreproduceable or legally unobtainable.**

INDEX